IMAGINE THAT!

Getting _Smarter_ Through Imagery Practice

Some comments...

"IMAGINE THAT! _makes using imagery for growth and awareness easy and fun...It does not tell the reader what to image but suggests how to develop such skills...Teachers, parents, human service professionals and social artists will find this book indispensable and it will be located in the 'users' section of their bookshelves._"

Marvin B. Sussman, Ph.D.
Unidel Professor of Human Behavior Emeritus
University of Delaware

"_Your book,_ IMAGINE THAT! _meets a real need of teachers and parents for guidance in utilizing guided imagery with children to develop higher order thinking skills and to empower those with alternate learning styles to succeed...I look forward to using the book in my classes and recommending it to students and faculty here at USC_"

Carol Flake, Ph.D.
Associate Professor, Instruction and Teacher Education, USC Columbia

"_Your book is a much needed addition to the field of education!..._IMAGINE THAT! _provided my graduate students with the scientific basis of imagery and its relationship to (our) course objectives. It provided first hand accounts of real teachers using imagery to understand their own learning/growth process, as well as, using imagery to enhance the learning/growth process of their students. It is especially powerful the way_ IMAGINE THAT! _relates the imagery exercises to Gardner's intelligences and the content areas. This aspect of_ IMAGINE THAT! _will make using imagery very easy for the novice of imagery in the classroom._"

Marcy Guddemi, Ph.D.
Assistant Professor of Early Childhood Education & Parent

"IMAGINE THAT! _is a delightful book that is very positive and applicable to the practice in classrooms across this country. Giving teachers the tools to help students visualize information and ways to learn is critical if we are to be successful in schools today. Tapping the great resource of the mind and its ability to develop and use information is, and must be, a major focus of the new processes that must develop in education for us to be successful with children from all cultural backgrounds and also with those of very radical different learning styles._"

Donna G. Dunning
Assistant Executive Director
Instruction/Human Relations & Parent

D1564724

IMAGINE THAT!

Getting *Smarter*
Through Imagery Practice

A Book For Teachers, Parents and Children

Lane Longino Waas, Ph.D.

J

JALMAR PRESS
Rolling Hills Estates, California

Library of Congress Catalog Card Number: 90-63767

Library of Congress Cataloging-in-Publication Data

Waas Ph.D., Lane Longino
    IMAGINE THAT! Getting Smarter Through Imagery Practice

ISBN 0-915190-71-0

Copyright © 1991 by Lane Longino Waas, Ph.D.

Published by Jalmar Press
45 Hitching Post Drive, Bldg. 2
Rolling Hills Estates, California 90274
Tel: (213) 547-1240

First edition
Printing: 10   9   8   7   6   5   4   3   2   1

Edited by Kathleen McMaster
Design & Composition by Charles E. Simpson
Manufactured in the United States of America

DEDICATION

I dedicate this book to my husband, Bill Waas

and

especially to Wilder McCullough and Katharine Hilburn,
our infant granddaughters.

To all of you, I dedicate my images of what is possible.

ACKNOWLEDGEMENTS

I thank you who helped me to remember my images: Many inspiring teachers, fellow-students at the Foundation for Brain and Mind Research, my art students of all ages, the teacher-volunteers of my doctoral research, and especially my community of friends who are my adult imagery groups.

Special thanks to:

Karen Holt, principal of the Montessori School of Anderson, South Carolina, and Ann Melton, curriculum coordinator for the Blue Ridge School of Cashiers, North Carolina, for allowing us to take photographs of their beautiful children.

Emil Fray, photographer, for his sensitive photographs.

Kathleen McMaster, my editor, who molded my thoughts and feelings into clearer word-images.

Bradley Winch, who envisioned that the publication of <u>Imagine That!</u> would be helpful to adults and to the children in their care.

John, for getting the process started.

George, for believing in me.

Sue and David, Lisa and Brian, Skip and Susie, and Ann, my children; Vicki and Mike, and Joe, my step-children; for continuing support.

Mom and Dad, who never doubted.

and to God, who "imagined us and created us in His own image."[1]

Lane Longino Waas

CONTENTS

Photographs that appear throughout this book were taken by Emil Fray, photographer, Cashiers, North Carolina.

EVOLUTION OF AN IMAGE

As a rule, indeed, grown-up people are fairly correct on matters of fact; it is in the higher gift of imagination that they are so sadly to seek.   Kenneth Grahame

I wish I thought their changes were just because of me! But I've been doing the same things, only the imagery practice is new. I wish I'd known this years ago!   an imagery research participant

My Journey (or, how this book came about)

Many wise teachers and friends assisted and advised me on my imagery journey. That journey led me into many courses, workshops, studies and, finally, into and through a doctoral program where I researched imagery for myself.

At the beginning of my journey, I was an art teacher and supervisor. For sixteen years, I observed and wondered at the spontaneous art-making abilities of young children. My youngest students drew and painted with a sureness of content, composition and color unparalleled in older children, teens or adults. Only those older individuals labeled as "creative" seemed to possess the same confidence in art-making. "Where does this art-making ability of young children come from," I wondered, "and where does it go as they grow older?"

I noticed that the children I worked with seemed to know or see *in total* or *in advance* what they were painting. That kind of seeing has been reported by numerous adult artists. For example, Michaelangelo claimed he saw the figure that he was to carve before he even touched the marble slab. His task, as he saw it, was to release the figure by carving away the stone which was *not* the figure. Although my young students were less articulate in describing their plans, they explained well enough for me to understand that a framework for their art existed.

I thought perhaps the children's natural ability to image was the driving force behind their early artistic expressions. After all, didn't their artistic abilities seem to decline as they developed verbal skills? I began to ask myself, "Is there a possibility that children could maintain the ability to think in images, even as verbal capacity increases? How could that happen? What would the result be?"

Interestingly, many of my skillful young art students were part of an academic group labeled "dyslexic." Why? My curiousity led me to graduate school in 1976 to both satisfy my interest in dyslexic students and to learn how better to assist in their learning. At that time there was a new (to me) theory circulating that the human brain was composed of two hemispheres which functioned differently. One seemed to prefer visual, spatial information coding. My initial response was, "How absolutely wonderful!" Although I could not explain my enthusiastic, intuitive response to something then so sketchily explained, I was sure that within it was the key to helping my dyslexic students.

However, since this particular brain research was generally regarded with skepticism, I put aside my immediate interest in it. Then, in 1979, when Betty Edward's book, <u>Drawing on the Right Side of the Brain</u>, was published, I became ecstatic! It made complete sense to me. My interest in right brain research and practice quickly renewed — I could hardly wait to begin teaching from this method! Although the theories were still regarded with suspicion by many of my colleagues, the processes based on them appeared to work. I witnessed the return to spontaneity and *seeing* my older students had demonstrated as young children in my class. Parents started attending the classes, so I began teaching a class after school for those adults who wanted to rediscover their own creative processes.

My excitement increasing, I flew to Seattle to attend a seminar taught by Dr. Joseph Bogen who co-authored work with Nobel scientist Dr. Roger Sperry on split brain research. I was to return often because of the energetic explosion of ideas there not yet being expressed in the South. Through the Seattle-based international network, New Horizons for Learning, I learned of, sought out and worked with theorists who encouraged my exploration of imagistic thought. I also attended a Berkely seminar taught by mind-body expert Kenneth Pelletier and mythologist Joseph Campbell. Then followed three years of working with "Renaissance woman" Dr. Jean Houston, bodywork expert Robert Masters and energy psychologist Gay Luce, all at the Foundation of Brain and Mind Research. All of my experience to date had convinced me that there are multiple ways of thinking, learning, and seeing the world. I wanted more experiences and insight into imagery and related fields. But how? My quest continued.

I attended an educational conference in Tarrytown, NY where I explored other new ideas, including Howard Gardner's ground-breaking work with multiple intelligences, Bob Samples' work with creativity and Tom Roberts' work with states of consciousness education. Too, as I had become exceptionally involved in Betty Edwards' work with visual training and creativity — having already taught with her methods — I further pursued her findings, reinforcing my own developing images. Tony Buzan's mind-mapping intrigued me since it offered graphic representation of visual thinking which differed from traditional methods of thought organization. These many new educational approaches helped me continue to believe that my *dyslexic* children were capable and intelligent in their own ways. Interacting with these innovative thinkers and researchers gave me the energy and courage to continue to believe that there were creative new methods and processes that would guide me in helping such students to *unlock* their abilities.

There were more experiences to come for me. Leading adult groups in applications of current brain and mind research, while maintaining a detailed journal, were important components of my graduate work with Dr. Houston. For five years, I designed weekly sessions in "Personal Growth and Community Building." In the process, I discovered the incredible part played by imagistic thought in the development of what was being called "the right brain."

The changes observed in participants were remarkable. My own personal growth while leading these groups was equally incredible to me. As students, we were learning to use more of our thinking capacities, resulting in our feeling more self-confident, more creative and more caring as individuals and as group members. "How is this possible?" I wondered, but did not doubt the truth of it at all!

I began using stress management techniques involving imagery with my students at school. I added these same techniques when working with their parents who took my adult drawing classes. At first, both students and parents thought the processes strange but, within a very brief time, they would prompt me if I had forgotten to start the classes with a session on imagery. My students talked about their images, sharing what was occurring in their imagery and asking me for books and more information on the subject. Participants appeared more satisfied with themselves, and seemed happier and more able to relate to each other.

The next step on my imagery journey involved Psychosynthesis training for a year. Psycho**synthesis,** unlike analysis, unifies one's mind/body/spirit. Its primary teaching mode is imagery. As I studied the processes developed by Italian psychiatrist Roberto Assagioli, I recognized many of them from both my childhood ways of thinking, and from my adult experiences. I became convinced to pursue imagery work with children.

If imagery worked well, as it had for me, my groups, my students and their parents, how could I gain the knowledge to explain it in ways that were clear and helpful? That question led me to graduate school once again and into further imagery research.

Through my research, I began wholeheartedly to believe that young children naturally use imagery. To make imagery part of educational practice, it seemed it ought to occur first in early childhood — at an age when it is a natural, organic process. I also believed that, if teachers found imagery practice beneficial for themselves, they would realize how helpful it could be for the children they taught. After several years of working with parents and children, I designed my research study to test my beliefs, to uncover more about imaging and to determine how such findings might be applied by teachers everywhere.

As I began my research, the important role to be played by parents in the development and implementation of imagery became evident to me. So, I offer this book to all: to parents, teachers, the children of our schools and to our families everywhere.

INTRODUCTION

*I can give you nothing that has not already
its being within yourself. I can throw open
to you no picture gallery but your own...I help
you to make your own world visible. That is all.*
                                        Herman Hesse

To imagine is everything.
                                        Anatole France

*Yes, beliefs can be changed, lives can be altered,
deeds can be accomplished...gradually, or in a sudden
stroke...by a procedure so simple that most people
do not believe it until they are somehow persuaded
to try it.*   Harmon and Rheingold

The "it" referred to in the book, <u>Higher Creativity</u> (Harmon and Rheingold, 1984) is imagery, a primary mode of thinking. Imagistic thought uses the senses to produce images. That is, images may be seen, heard or created through any of the senses. Imagery practice is not new. It was, to quote Harmon and Rheingold, "our first and oldest way of describing the world to ourselves and others." Its reemergence in the realm of education follows successful practice in fields such as sports and medicine.

Olympic athletes of various disciplines demonstrated the successful use of imagery during televised segments of the recent Olympic games, when they practiced their skills using imagery prior to performance. A coach and counselor, who was a co-student of mine at the Foundation for Brain and Mind Research, related the enormous increase in skill development by his high school basketball team after practicing free throws in imagery. Karen, one of my research volunteers, saw tremendous improvement in the physical control and athletic abilities of her young, motor-disabled students when she used imagery exercises to help them perform.

The list of medical practitioners who use imagery with patients and write about its benefits is long. I participated in a workshop taught by one of these innovative individuals, Bernie Siegal, author of the popular <u>Love, Medicine and Miracles</u> (1986). A few others whose studies are well worth investigating are Herbert Benson (1975), O. Carl Simonton and Stephanie Matthews-Simonton (1978) and Jeanne Achterberg (1985.) Achterberg helped the Simontons in their early work with cancer patients.

Educational research powerfully validates imagery's usefulness to parents, teachers and students. In 1964, R.R. Holt published an article in American Psychologist, titled "Imagery: the Return of the Ostracized." In it he explained how imagery had been eliminated from areas deemed appropriate for scientific study while behaviorism reigned as the accepted Western scientific view. He continued by stating that internal processes, including imagery, are now seen by the scientific community as a valid part of human experience and these experiences are now sought after to provide material for current research.

The legitimization of imagery for scientific study by the naturalistic approach of cognitive science allowed it to become a focus of exploration once again. Cognitive science is based upon efforts to answer questions about human knowledge. It postulates that images (and other representations such as symbols and rules) exist in the human mind. The existence of such representation is necessary in order "to explain the variety of human behavior, action and thought."[1]

Because imagery is a natural way of thinking, human beings used it long before they learned to speak language. But, somehow, we seem to have lost the knack of practicing imagery and must now learn to re-access this powerful natural process. Many questions must be asked. For example, how may parents learn about imagery to use it for their personal growth and awareness? How may they use imagery to encourage the development of their children? How may teachers learn about imagery so they have the skills to design imagery exercises that will help their students succeed?

This book is designed to answer those questions. Some answers have come from my years of experience with imagery and some from my doctoral research. My studies centered on the use of imagery by insightful, caring teachers — the so-called "average" teachers of our schools. This book reveals their hopes for building a quality educational future through cooperative efforts in imagery practices.

Education, at its best, gives each person the tools to create a good life filled with purpose and integrity. We, as parents and teachers, dream of that kind of wholeness and richness for our children. If we experience new insights while guiding them, our lives also improve. When we consciously enter the practice of imagery, we allow ourselves to discover wonder, mystery and wholeness. When we create meaningful learning experiences for our children, we take large strides toward structuring a responsible stewardship for a quality future.

I am grateful for my studies in Early Childhood and Teacher Education. Through the life-span focus of that program I was able to realize how imagery practice is the best and most fruitful way for families and educators to learn to work together.

The section of this book called "Imagination and Learning" contains exercises applicable to a variety of subject matter, addressing areas of emphasis at home and within the school curriculum. Appearing in a form which may be directly used, they may also be easily adapted to any particular group of students or situations. These exercises are supported by Howard Gardner's brilliant work, Frames of Mind, which defines a broad range of human gifts he refers to as intelligences. Dr. Gardner, a developmental psychologist and Professor of Education at Harvard University's Graduate School of Education, is the first American to receive the $150,000 University of Louisville Grawemeyer Award in Education. His work first indicates his belief that human intelligence has been incompletely defined and narrowly educated, then identifies seven different kinds of intelligence discussed thoroughly in a later section of this book. In his work, he postulates that the key to a happy and productive life rests in identifying and using those intelligences with which people can be most creative. Co-director of Harvard's Project Zero, a research group that studies human intelligence, Dr. Gardner has a positive reaction to the imagery exercises in Imagine That! which show, he says, "that each human intelligence has its own imaginative forms."

The section of the book called "Research into Imagery" provides a scientifically-based foundation for the use of imagery. The material in this section covers exactly what imagery practice can accomplish in the home, workplace and classroom and why its application is so important in human development.

As I continue my research in the field of imagistic thought, I ask that you share what you find to be helpful with me, as well as with others. You are my best research participants! I appreciate any feedback you may be willing to give me. Thank you in advance!

My vision is that this book will guide you into an understanding of the natural mind-process called imagery. My dream is that you may find this book to be so exciting and beneficial that you will share it with your family, friends and all those children whose lives you touch. I now offer you with my images of a natural educational process that meets the important needs of students, teachers, administrators, parents, and the community.

RESEARCH INTO IMAGERY

Make our...enjoyment of the things that feed
the mind as aware of itself as possible,
since that awareness quickens the mental
demand...This is the very education of our
imaginative life.
                                    Henry James

The teacher is indeed wise...who does not bid you
enter the house of his wisdom, but rather leads you
to the threshold of your own mind.
                                    Kahlil Gibran

If I gave you a magic wand with which you could transform children's education into your vision of the ideal, what kind of changes and results would you desire? Take a few minutes to list those important changes and results.

When I asked groups of teachers and other adults this question, they assembled lists ranging from improved behavior and higher test scores to developed creativity and greater motivation.

People who use imagery have discovered that practicing it at home and in the classroom can create many beneficial results! Later in this section, you can examine a list of results which parents and teachers noted for *themselves* through imagery practice.

Categories of Beneficial Change for Children

Through the use of imagery, teachers and researchers have observed children to have:

1. Increased Enthusiasm
2. Better Self-Esteem
3. Improved Memory Skills
4. Greater Respect for Self and Others
5. Improved Health
6. Greater Mental Flexibility
7. Expanded Imagination, Creativity and Intuition
8. Improved Thinking Skills
9. Increased Autonomy
10. More Control Over Personal Behavior
11. Improved Self-Expression
12. Increased Ability to Relax
13. Better Listening Skills
14. Improved Motor Skills
15. Stronger Social Skills
16. Higher Levels of Personal Satisfaction

Now, let's examine each of these categories independently. References to individuals (Kathy, Lisa and Karen) refer to participants in my imagery research. Their work is clarified later in this chapter and in the chapter, "Stories and Images." Children who use imagery are found to have:

1. Increased Enthusiasm

Third grade teacher Kathy told me, "It just tickles me to see the children now. They're excited about learning!" Karen agrees when she says, "Learning seems to be a part of them now. They're interested in learning! That's why I'm excited about teaching again!" Parents say they are relieved and pleased when their children seem motivated by their excitement about learning! Many teachers have told me they have students whom they know could learn if only the children could become excited about learning. Teachers and parents alike will attest to the rewards of helping children who are enthusiastic about learning! Such motivation, enthusiasm and excitement are readily evident in children after imagery practice.

2. Better Self-Esteem

"Annie's mother is really pleased by her daughter's response to imagery practice," Kathy reported. "She says Annie loves it and that it seems to make her feel secure."

"Secure" and "confident" are words most often used to describe children who regularly use imagery. A large body of data$_1$ suggests that self-esteem lies at the base of a child's ability to learn. Many states are currently adopting extensive plans to study and implement self-esteem within the learning environment, showing how this finding is more important than ever! Children with healthy images of themselves, those who feel secure and confident, are more free to learn and less restricted by fears of failure and personal doubts.

3. Improved Memory Skills

I have seen high school students, who are often reticent with their responses, laughing with pleasure as they learn new ways to remember assigned information. They have told me imagery is really helpful to them! Imagery exercises enhance the ability to remember, creating better, more skillful learners. These abilities decrease the time needed to learn the vast amounts of material required to increase knowledge and understanding in today's world.

4. Greater Respect for Self and Others

The results of imagery practice with the students of the volunteers in my study were often profound in their implications. Kathy's observation that her students were no longer fighting was an outstanding example. "We've become a little community," she told me. "This is our family now."

Through imagery, students learn cooperation, balancing the competitive drive already in place. Students develop an appreciation for the differences among a group of people, recognizing the riches their diversity brings to the whole. Children and adults may learn to notice, some for the first time, good traits in individuals they had previously disliked. As such outwardly directed respect/appreciation develops, family relationships also tend to improve.

5. Improved Health

My daughter, paraplegic as the result of an automobile accident, has practiced imagery to improve her muscle control and to overcome infections. A young girl I saw on television said she had suffered from migraine headaches before she began using imagery. She reported that her use of imagery and related techniques had enabled her to call on her body's own healing processes. She now controls her headaches through continued use of such procedures.

What a boon it would be if all children, through imagery practice, learned at an early age to manage and maintain their wellness! A number of physicians — with demonstrated success — already encourage young, critically ill patients to take an active part in their own recovery.

Children, by using positive mental images, can learn to improve their health when ill and stay healthier for longer periods of time.

6. Greater Mental Flexibility

Most scientists no longer believe that there is just one natural state of consciousness. Their investigations suggest that we have a variety of internal states, (alert, drowsy, dreaming, etc.) and that skills are state-specific. Specific abilities may be attainable through the accessing of particular states of mind. For example, I may not be able to solve a math problem in a day-dreaming state; however, in that state I may discover an idea that leads to a solution for a compositional problem. Creative geniuses, Einstein and Mozart among them, have done exactly that.

7. Expanded Imagination, Creativity and Intuition

I taught art to children of all ages for almost twenty years. During those years, I noticed that as children clarified their images through art production, they were able to access their imaginations, creative processes and intuitive capacities. As children rediscover their creativity and intuition, classrooms come alive! Education in the recent past ignored several important areas of research. Now, though, the value of

KATHY'S CHART

This was designed to show the remarkable increase in Kathy's science student's grades after beginning to use imagery exercises previous to test-taking. The chart illustrates changes over a six week time span. The column "Science Grades without Imagery Exercises" lists grades averaged from the six weeks before beginning imagery practice in the classroom (See page 42 for discussion).

GRADES	SCIENCE GRADES w/o IMAGERY	SCIENCE GRADES with IMAGERY					
		Week 1	2	3	4	5	6
A	2	7	14	14	10	13	14
B	1	5	2	0	5	0	0
C	2	2	1	3	0	2	1
D	3	2	0	0	1	0	1
F	9	1	0	0	0	0	0

NOTES:
1. In WEEK 1, the "F" grade was scored by the one student who was not participating in the imagery exercise.
2. In WEEK 2, the "D" grade was scored by one student who came to class late and missed the imagery exercise before taking.the test.
3. In WEEK 6, the "D" grade was scored by one student who was called out of the classroom and missed the imagery exercise before taking the test.

The exercise used previous to each test was a simple relaxation exercise.

creativity and intuition studies is receiving acknowledgement. For example, Benjamin Bloom's structure for the cognitive, affective and physical domains, used in teaching since the mid-1950's, has been joined by a classification for intuitive knowledge, developed by Zoa Rockenstein in 1985. Rockenstein's research shows the strong relationship between intuition, imagination, creativity and a child's higher level thinking skills.

8. Improved Thinking Skills

I have often observed that children engaged in "higher level thinking," are more able than others to make quality choices regarding important life issues. Parents have the right and responsibility to teach their children what has value for them. But it is through learning how to examine what parents and teachers have taught them that young people are able to form their own value systems. Benjamin Bloom, an educational theorist, notes, when explaining thinking skills, that simple recitation of memorized material is not high level thinking. Researchers[1] observe that children who use imagery move into expanded and higher realms of thinking, exhibit increased mastery of specific cognitive materials and score higher on tests. Imagery practice provides a natural, cost-free means to achieve these goals.

9. Increased Autonomy

When my older art students, who were practicing imagery, became aware of the social issue of hunger, they got personally involved in taking action to help feed people. Their imagery enhanced their abilities to examine themselves and their secure places in the world, and enabled them to recognize the needs of others as well as to take action. Their efforts were so successful and innovative that an Atlanta television station filmed them and presented the students to the community as models of what young people could accomplish when they began to be aware of the world beyond themselves.

Parents and educators believe that it is only as children are able to define themselves in relationship to peers, family, community and the larger environment that they are able to develop their own values and reach toward their full potential. Abraham Maslow (1971) wrote that a human must attain a developed self-awareness before approaching an ability to focus beyond himself into the world. Children using imagery display greater autonomy and express more self-awareness because of imagery-developed affective understanding.

10. More Control Over Personal Behavior

Parents and teachers have shared with me "how much better" their children act following imagery practice. Good behavior in the classroom is a major goal of educators. It's an extremely important factor affecting quality learning. Self-control is a necessity for children in order for them to grow into happy, well-adjusted citizens. As children become more responsible for their thinking and learning, they develop self-control in all areas of communication, at home as well as at school. Imagery practice develops a child's ability to control his or her behavior.

11. Improved Self-Expression

Lisa's daughter Georgia, (four years old at the time) expressed her feelings uniquely when she told her mother that she had been sad, "but my sad ran into the ground like the water from the hose." Georgia, a regular practitioner of imagery, often expresses herself imagistically. She created a drawing, reproduced later in the book, which expresses her feelings of being safe and comfortable during her earliest imagery practice, when she described not seeing "anything but black."

In "Steps for Guiding Imagery Exercises," discussed in the chapter called "Imagination and Learning: Exercises," Beverly Galyean defines expression as a necessary step within the imagery process. Parents and teachers have often related their fears that expression will lead to chaos. The practice of imagery, though, offers children ways to express thoughts and feelings that are appropriate to the learning environment and to the individual child. Children who practice imagery are both expressive and self-disciplined.

12. Increased Ability to Relax

I've noticed many children in my classes who appeared fearful before taking a test. After engaging in an imagery exercise, their relaxation, confidence and mental focus were evident and as a result they achieved higher scores than when previously tested. I asked three young children who were preparing to take standardized tests, "Why do you do imagery exercises before beginning testing?" "It relaxes us," they responded. "It makes it easier to do," one added.

Clench your fist tightly, then release it. Feel the warm tingle as the oxygenated blood returns to your hand and fingers. To function optimally, your hand and fingers require unrestricted blood flow. Internal processes have much the same need. If children experience stress, their muscles tighten, blood flow, and thus oxygen supply, is inhibited and they cannot perform optimally. But, when they learn to relax through imagery, physiological changes occur that allow children to learn with greater ease.

13. Better Listening Skills

A teacher told me she wished she had an hour's vacation for each time she said to students, "Listen now," or asked, "Are you listening now?" Parents have told me many similar tales. Children learn to listen carefully as they are guided in imagery exercises. They enjoy the exercises and they pay attention to what is being said. Better listening skills learned in imagery often transfer to other subjects and other situations.

14. Improved Motor Skills

Karen, one of the volunteers in my doctoral study, created videotapes which demonstrated a remarkable improvement by her students following imagery exercises. One motor-impaired child "improved fifty-to-ninety percent," she reported. "It was just incredible!"

Imagery use increases the ability of children who are motor-impaired to control body movements. Children with more normal physical conditions who practice imagery develop an unusually high level of motor skills and excel at specific athletic activities.

15. Stronger Social Skills

Children, like adults, develop a sense of community as a result of imagery practice. As Kathy (another volunteer from my research group) stated earlier in this text, children cease fighting and get along better when they use imagery. Group work, necessary for building social skills, becomes a pleasure rather than a chore.

This category builds upon previously mentioned benefits. As children become more secure (Benefit Number Two), they are observed to be less defensive as they work with others in groups. As they develop respect for others (Benefit Number Four), they generate an atmosphere of sharing and learning which allows them to cooperate with one another as they work together.

16. Higher Levels of Personal Satisfaction

If children are happy, they have a positive attitude toward the learning process and exhibit enthusiasm for the future. Although "happy" is difficult to define, people recognize it when they experience it. The teachers with whom I have worked report greater job satisfaction and greater happiness in all aspects of their lives because of their imagery practice. Quantities of research[1] relate observations that children who use imagery are happier than those who do not. We as parents are happier, too, when our children are satisfied.

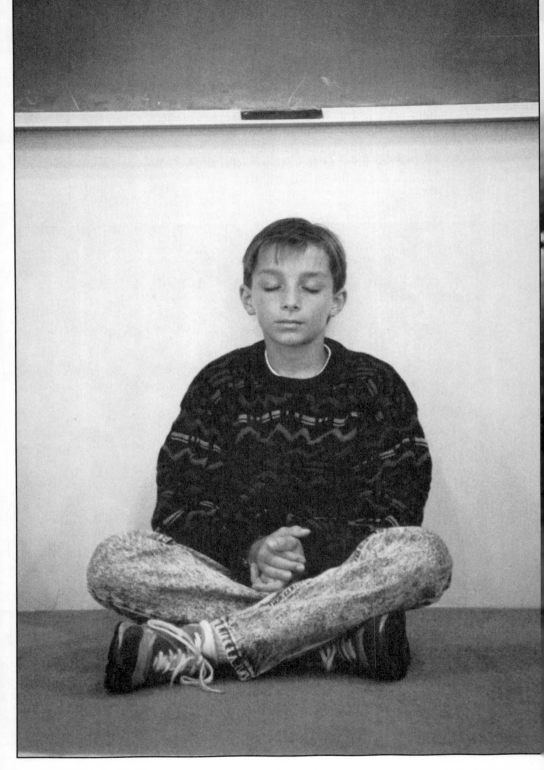

Imagistic Thought Development

The fact is that *all young children first think in images*. As children develop the ability to speak in words, this new skill need not inhibit their original ability to image. Verbal and imagistic thought systems are separate yet complementary, enhancing one another in performance. Today, quality education for children should include training in images as well as in words.

I believe that many discoveries await us as we begin to regain and develop our natural abilities to think in images. It is possible that imagery development, through a synergistic process, will more than double a child's individual access to new ways of thinking. It is not too late for adults to recall and enjoy their imagistic abilities as they use them to enhance awareness and expand their access to a wide range of thinking processes.

Since children are born with the capacity to imagize and to verbalize, it is we teachers and parents who must reactivate *our* capacities to think in images. We can then include the image as well as the word when teaching our children.

Imagery is an inherent thinking process, but because it was unused and undeveloped for several generations, the educational system needs to implement programs now to provide information about imagery and instruction in its use. The use of imagery as a foundational building block which supports innovative educational reform is too important a process to remain in research laboratories. Children need imagery exercises in their classrooms now!

Imagery is a way of thinking that requires introspection. It involves the senses like lenses that focus upon images. Jeanne Achterberg (1985) expands that definition by stating that imagery "is the communication mechanism between perception, emotion and bodily change." Imagery includes, but is not limited to visualization. Images may be *seen, heard* and *felt*. Notice that the sense of *smell* registers some images and *taste* records images as well. A person thinking intuitively might describe his or her imagery experience by saying, "I sense the images." When parents and teachers can determine which sense or senses their children most often use to perceive images, they will have a greater understanding of how learning occurs. When adults can identify children's individual styles of learning or intelligences, (as defined by Howard Gardner in <u>Frames of Mind</u>) they may begin to see all children as gifted! It is a fact that many more children test as gifted after imagery practice.

You can identify the senses you use most often to receive images by noticing what happens if I tell you a large green alligator is crawling toward you. Perhaps you immediately *see* that creature in your mind and *feel* the image as fear. Your image may even trigger a kinesthetic (muscle) image as you jump or quickly change positions. Imagine yourself standing, sitting or walking on your favorite beach. You may smell the salt air, feel the texture and the temperature of the sand or listen to the sounds of the sea birds as you hear the waves crashing upon the shore. Imagine having a freshly cut lemon half placed in your hand. What do you experience?

If the large majority of your images are visual, I could infer that you are a visual thinker and your primary style of learning could be identified as visual-spatial. I would then be appropriate in providing you with as many opportunities for visual learning as I could create. If you had few visual images and most of your images were kinesthetic or muscular in nature, I would create an environment in which you could move about as you learn — in fact to learn through movement. Your primary style of learning could be identified as kinesthetic.

When learning styles and *intelligences* are identified in this manner, it is possible to make quality learning experiences available to all children. Only the boundaries of human imagination limit the variety of ways imagery practice can be used.

Listening to Some Experts

Educational reform is one of today's most compelling issues. The study of human thought moved to the forefront of inquiry during the last decade and the impact of the discovery of new thinking processes has created an intense demand for educational change. If, as studies[1] indicate, people think more broadly and deeply than was once believed possible, then children must be encouraged to be aware of and to use those expanded thought processes.

Morton Hunt[2] states that cognitive scientists, in less than a decade, have made remarkable progress in the discovery of how the mind works and how humans think. Prominent educational theorist Leslie Hart has expressed his belief that the integration of these discoveries will support "new learning theories of a scope and quality never before available."[3]

I agree with these theories of educational reform which affirm the beliefs that **change is necessary** and that **educational quality can be restored** through the application of knowledge gained from current brain and mind research.

Images are created by the person practicing imagery. Although images may be suggested, as illustrated in the section of this book called "Imagination and Learning," imagery practitioners construct their own images. The practice of imagery can be integrated into existing programs and curricula easily *because* imagery is self-constructed knowledge. Its use expands all ways of teaching and learning by introducing an awareness of internal processes to the participants. Imagery practice builds relationships between external sensations and internal awarenesses. Only those educational models narrowly built upon forms that do not allow critical thinking processes oppose imagery study, which is a cooperative, non-competitive educational process.

Aristotle wrote centuries ago, "thought is impossible without an image." Emmanuel Kant stated, "thinking in pictures precedes thinking in words." Albert Einstein (a visual and kinesthetic thinker who had to translate his images into words) said that the source of his thought was the interaction of images.

During the first half of the twentieth century, behaviorism prevailed as the western scientific view. Imagery, with its internal thought origins, was declared unsuitable for study and use at that time because scientists believed only external and observable processes were acceptable evidence for use in research. My hope is that this book will help place imagery research and practice within the reach of people everywhere.

Child and Adult Development

I have stated that imagery practice benefits children in specific ways. Yet, it may be helpful now to cite some experts in child development so that the importance of teaching imagery in the classroom can be seen even more clearly.

Educational giant Piaget, speaking about self-constructed reality, has well documented evidence to support his theory: verbal symbolism needs to be complemented by a system of imaginal symbols to represent completely what children comprehend. Applying this dual system in the classroom, Larry Greeson and Drea Zigarmi report in Humanistic Education and Development (vol. 24): "Mental imagery provides a potentially powerful alternative mode of symbolic representation for young children...as young as preschool and kindergarten age."

Numerous other scientists have reported observing strong relationships between healthy child development and creative, imagistic practice. Doug Stewart explored visual thinking with Stanford University professors and states in Smithsonian (August, 1985): "Young children do indeed seem to have active visual imaginations, and with practice, might be able to hang onto this ability...as they develop verbal skills."

Robert Rose, in <u>The Gifted Child Quarterly</u> (Vol. 23), reports the results of use of imagery in the classroom as: strong, upward movement in achievement scores, a higher percentage of gifted IQ scores than expected, levels-growth in academics, and improved behavior.

Howard Rheingold[4] says that children who develop pretending skills and play imaginatively tend to be happier and more involved in learning. He reports that imagination is a necessary component of enhanced human learning and that the capacity to adopt an attitude toward the possible (imaginary) may be "one of the highest human capacities." He ends by saying that "the establishment of a science of imagination is an important step in transforming our present educational system to meet the needs of a transforming society."

Educational theorist Jerome Singer offers parents and educators a genuine hope for the human possibilities to be discovered through the practice of imagery when he says: "By living life not only through immediate response or perception but by reduplicating experience, replaying past material, and trying out alternatives on the level of fantasy, we may be providing ourselves with a genuine freedom, a broader perspective, and indeed a broader life space on which to play out our term on earth."[5]

According to Kathryn Alesandrini in <u>Imagery in Education</u> (1985), *"The question is no longer whether or not mental imagery facilitates learning, but rather how it can best be used to produce the optimum faciliation."*

Categories of Beneficial Change
for Adults

Based upon my work with students of all ages, I have noticed those who engage in imagery practice experience many specific benefits. I began my investigations with the theory that change could be identified if imagery practice were to occur within a research study. I also believed that once parents and teachers identified those changes as beneficial they would want to pass them on to the children in their care. In my doctoral study, teacher-volunteers were asked to note any changes (positive or otherwise) that they recognized happening because of imagery. They were asked to clarify the nature of their responses by noting whether the changes were personal, including family interactions, or professional, involving the children in their classrooms. I have organized their responses into the following eight categories of beneficial change.

Through the practice of imagery, teacher-volunteers reported and were observed to demonstrate:

1. Increased Awareness
2. Expanded Creativity
3. Improved Self-Esteem
4. Greater Enthusiasm
5. More Intellectual and Emotional Flexibility
6. Enhanced Intuition
7. Increased Autonomy
8. Accelerated Personal Growth

1. Increased Awareness

I was surprised to notice how few of the participants had ever considered what, why or how they thought. As I watched several of my volunteers become aware of their thinking processes, I enjoyed seeing them display their delight with sparkling eyes and smiling faces and I loved listening to them express feelings of wonder at their new insight.

Lisa, a young mother, said that she had never been aware of the "voices that run around in my head" until she was asked to image and think about her thinking. Later she remarked "I just didn't pay attention to how I thought before this…I find when I'm listening now that I make images from what other people are telling me."

Early in the study, Kathy said she was "made more aware of her thinking and how we all use imagery and don't even know it!"

While using imagery with his young students, John recognized that "It's a way for them to mentally plan what they're going to do...to calm down...to collect themselves." Karen, commenting on imagery said, "I think it's self-awareness now, being more aware of what you think and how you think and what you can do to change it."

2. Expanded Creativity

The volunteers began to see new relationships between their thinking and their teaching as well as between their teaching and children's learning. As they began to recognize how their new awareness of their thinking could free them to begin to design fresh, innovative teaching methods they created a variety of inspired techniques using imagistic thought based upon brain and mind research.

People who study creativity have pointed out that individuals observed to be creative tend to be those who see themselves as creative. Dr. Jean Houston suggests that creative blocks are no more than blocks in the ability to image. As the teachers in my study began to image themselves as creative, they experienced a considerable increase in the creative aspects of their thinking.

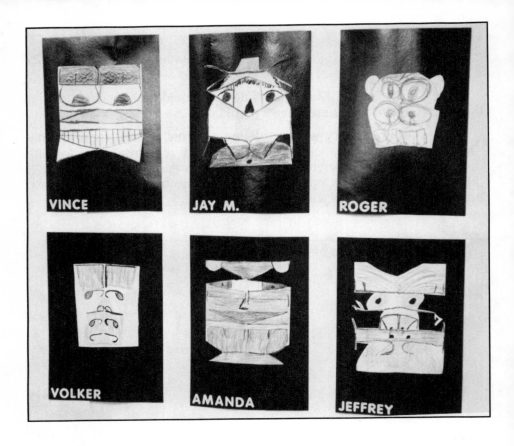

VINCE   JAY M.   ROGER

VOLKER   AMANDA   JEFFREY

John stated that through his use of imagery, "I'm more aware of what I've been doing, and by being aware, it's helping me to develop control and to be more creative."

Lisa's imagination and creativity were expressed in her lyrical response, "When I'm driving on the road to school, I seem to be just tuning into it more now…to the spirit of the road…to the poetry of it."

Pam's students expressed their reactions to her newly designed imagery exercises with drawings that illustrated how the children had moved beyond the stereotypical images often seen in elementary classrooms.

Karen designed and produced a series of videotapes of her children doing their movement exercises, both before and after imagery, in order to see more clearly the physical changes occurring because of imagistic practice.

Kathy became exceptionally creative in her applications of imagery in all aspects of the school curriculum. She recorded her students' verbal responses to specific exercises in their creative writing class. Kathy's audiotape supplements research studies that show children's writing skills to be of a much higher order following imagery exercises.[6]

3. Improved Self-Esteem

As I mentioned previously, self-esteem development appears to be one of the foundations of human behavior. When the teachers in my study improved their self-esteem with imagery, they gained new freedoms they had never before imagined. One of them remarked, "Self-concept is simply the image I have of myself!" Images are subject to individual control and they may be changed in any way wished or imagined.

Cathy said, "Imagery has affected my life more than I thought it could. It has made me think more positively. I'm sure this has affected my self-concept."

Lisa described her change of attitude in this way, "I think it was doing this imagery and seeing how we're all different that made me not take a friend's comment as a criticism of me. That is a big change!"

"The biggest improvement from this imagery work is my own self-esteem," Karen said. "I lacked self-esteem as a teacher. I've been able to relax and think about positive things I've done and not just the negative. My personal gains were the most important. Before this, I was limited in being able to help my students."

4. Greater Enthusiasm

Imagery practice is fun! Children and teachers alike enjoy it. Using imagery exercises provides new approaches to familiar materials which assist both students and teachers in accomplishing their goals. These new approaches empower teachers' personal creativity and autonomy and they become more excited about their jobs!

Cathy M. shared her excitement during a telephone call to my home when she announced her new enthusiasm over the success of an imagery exercise she had led for her children.

I asked Pam if she felt imagery practice was any help to her, and she replied, "Oh, yes! It gives a purpose, or reason, to my teaching!"

Kathy elaborated on this subject with several examples of her excitement about teaching with imagery: "I look forward to the subject areas. There are more hands-on-things after imagery and I love watching my students experience them! I'm just so tickled that they're pleased with it. Their grades are improving, too, and now they are feeling more and sensing more. It's great to see this happen!" I asked Kathy if she would use imagery after the project was over. "Oh yes! Definitely! I'll continue every year I'm teaching!" she replied. "I just love it! Since I've been involved with imagery, I'm more excited and I seem to be more creative in my teaching. I look forward to the next day of work."

5. More Intellectual and Emotional Flexibility

My volunteers shared their amazement as they became aware of their former ways of judging others' motives. They began to perceive other people differently, with more empathy and caring.

Pam (an art teacher) told me that the other teachers at her school held art education in low esteem. Because of imagery practice, she was able to accept their attitude as "the way it is" and subsequently began to do her best to understand *their* subjects and *their* ways of teaching. In response, they began to be supportive of her art program, making complimentary comments and attending student art exhibits more often.

In spite of her fears about using imagery, because it was not an integral part of her school's long-established curriculum, Karen began to use imagery applications in appropriate areas. She became able to examine the restrictions she had placed upon her thinking, and to come to the realization that, possibly, they need not exist at all. In referring to her broadened perceptions she stated, "Before imagery practice, I was limited in my ability to help my students."

Lisa shared stories about her increased empathy, which she attributed to the use of imagery. She told me about her ability to imagize her husband's stories concerning his early adventures in hunting. Now she can understand his current "hunting obsession" because she knows that its roots were formed by his youthful love and respect for the quiet, still woods. Previously, Lisa's response to her husband's "obsession" had created conflict and discomfort for her. Now, in her imagination, she could see and feel those things that made it so important to him. "It really made me a lot more empathetic," she admitted.

These teachers, filled with new perceptions of their thought processes and strengthened self-esteem, began to reexamine the feelings and ideas they had about some of the people with whom they worked or lived and through that process, began to acknowledge and accept the validity of different points of view.

6. Enhanced Intuition

Dr. Zoa Rockenstein clearly defined the intuitive domain in her 1985 doctoral dissertation. She remarked on the fact that American education has rarely included the study of intuition. Frances Vaughn[7] called imagery "the language of intuition." She explained that learning to understand imagery's language is a necessary step in the process of expanding intuition.

Beverly Galyean (a pioneer of educational imagery) said, "Imagery is both the fabric and design of intuition. It is the universal language of direct knowing and direct perception, both of which are aspects of intuitive intelligence."

I was not able to document my theory that the use of imagery practice would create an awareness of increased intuition. Since American schools rarely teach courses involving intuitive intelligence, the teachers in my study had little or no awareness of their initial intuition, so lacked a gauge to measure improvement.

Both Pam and Cathy M. said that initially they experienced a lack of awareness of intuition. John found intuition difficult to describe and Lisa informed me that her intuitive abilities, although natural to her, had "become expanded from learning about imagery." She, too, stated, "I had just never thought about it before." Karen told me she was becoming more flexible when she responded to her children and was paying more attention to her "hunches" now.

7. Increased Autonomy

Constance Kamii[8] identified Piaget's aim of education as moral and intellectual autonomy (being governed by oneself.) Jacob Bronowski, in a Yale University publication[9], revealed his finding that autonomy is the ability to visualize [image] alternatives and make choices between them. Leslie Hart wrote, in a 1986 article in <u>Phi Delta Kappan,</u> that when teachers in his study were first asked to take control of the design of their teaching, (to "visualize alternatives and make choices between them") they were unable to proceed. After years of having followed set curricula and established methods, they were unable to begin designing original teaching material. It may seem difficult at first to change from passively teaching, using set guidelines, to actively helping establish strategies. However, after only a few weeks of working with imagery, the teachers in my study began to show more control over their teaching, choice-making and even their physical health.

Karen had struggled through many diets and exercise regimes with little success. When she began to use imagery, she lost weight. Lisa used imagery to stop smoking and John continues to use imagery to manage stress. Once he became aware of his personal images, he learned he could choose to create positive, rather than negative images.

When Kathy created new methods to teach the use of imagery, she moved beyond strengthening her own autonomy and began to encourage and empower her students. Kathy declared, "I want them to be able to use imagery without me. I want them to learn that it is something they have with them all the time and to learn to be on their own with it. I want them to use it at home, to be independent with their imagery."

8. Accelerated Personal Growth

Dr. Jean Houston stated that, since "the brain, mind, body and emotions are intricately connected, to extend one is to extend another." This idea was demonstrated during my imagery study when the volunteers shared how they had experienced growth and development simultaneously in several areas of their lives. The heightened awareness of their thinking processes resulted in increased self-awareness. Self-esteem development multiplied their number of autonomous behaviors.

There was a notable increase in the satisfaction level of the teachers in my study because of imagery practice. By gaining more control over their lives through increased autonomy, these teachers began to recognize the possibility of enacting the changes necessary to improve their personal situations. This was the turning point in the study when they began to express more satisfaction with their personal and professional lives. They told me they had gained more emotional flexibility and said they were not becoming as easily angered or frustrated. They also expressed an awareness of having a far greater range of feelings with the means to express them.

The benefits described in the previous eight categories emphasize the importance of teachers and parents reaccessing their image-making capacities. It is when their learning is undertaken that the children will benefit. Helping our children make extraordinary gains in educational and life skills is an unequalled gift. Some call it educational reform. Educational giant Uri Bronfenbrenner[10] calls it "a curriculum for caring." I call it love.

STORIES AND IMAGES

*I am always fascinated with images, particularly
as they speak to our relationship to God. There is
no other way to speak about God but by images. So,
I invite you to 'play with' new images to talk about
God and life and yourself.
What is God like to you?...Sort of like a singing clown?
Like a crying old man ?...Like a magnificent silver
rocket ?..A summer storm?
God is not any of these. God is like them, and others,
and others, and others. The way you image God will
say a lot about how you relate to God, and on that may
depend your fundamental faith.*
the Rev. Harry Pritchett

In this section, three of the volunteers in my research study tell their stories. Although they were led in an imagery exercise at each meeting and provided books and other written resources, they were neither taught imagery nor told how to use it. Their different responses show some of the results of imagery practice and display a variety of approaches to imagery.

Karen, a parent and teacher, chose to use imagery with her motor disabled students and for personal goals as well. She made videotapes of her students so their physical movements before and after imagery could be compared. Her uses of imagery promoted the development of the Kinesthetic, Visual-Spatial, and Personal Intelligences of her children. *Lisa* is a mother of two children who plans to return to teaching when her newborn child is older. She chose emotional and social uses for imagery and applied them to herself and with her family. Her uses of imagery promoted the development of Intrapersonal Intelligence, Interpersonal Intelligence, and Musical Intelligence. *Kathy*, a teacher of young children, developed countless ways to use imagery within the school curriculum. She kept improvement charts so she and I could see the progress made by her students during a semester of imagery practice. She also made audiotapes of the children talking about their images and how to use them in writing. Kathy's goal was to teach imagery in such a way that her children knew it was something they always had with them. She wanted to teach them that they could use imagery in every way imaginable. Her uses of imagery promoted the development of the Verbal-Linguistic, Logical-Mathmatical, and Intrapersonal Intelligences.

The personal intelligences are noted here more often than others. A healthy self-esteem is the basis for learning. Developing the personal intelligences by using imagery is the best way to accomplish the goal of achieving healthy self-esteem.

On the following pages, the volunteers of my study will tell you, in their own words, what it was like to agree to participate in a study using imagery when they were not familiar with it. They will share with you their ideas about imagery at the start of the project and how the focus of their work developed during imagery practice. They will share with you as well, what kind of changes took place in their lives and the lives of those around them because of imagery practice. Open yourself to their stories, if you will. The process of imagery can work just as easily for you and your children.

LISA

"When I first used imagery, I thought it was just something you did in your mind, just visual images. I'd heard of imagery. My dad is a therapist and I guess I had heard him mention it. But I'd never tried it before I volunteered for this project.

It was funny at first, because there were no rules. I was told just to do some imagery exercises and to see what happened. I had to check out books to find out how to do them! I kept notes on which imagery exercises I used and a journal about my experiences. But, at first, I had no idea where these things would lead me! No idea at all!

We'd get together during class break and talk about our experiences, and talking about them seemed to sharpen them for me. All my images, particularly sound and touch, became more vivid. I guess that is because I'm paying attention to them now. As I said, I'd thought images were all visual. Not mine! Oh, I can see an image when I try, but I can feel the image too, like I'm in my body in the picture. It's being away from it, looking in and also being in it at the same time! They're really interesting to me as I notice them more now. I find that when I'm listening, I make pictures of what other people are telling me. I just didn't pay attention to how I thought before this."

KATHY

"I'm really enthusiastic about this imagery practice! I did not even dream of what it was before. I just thought it had something to do with your imagination. Oh, it does, but much more, too. It involves all my senses. Daydreaming is imagery, too, and so is role-playing.

I had an idea of what I hoped imagery would do, though. I wanted to find a way for the children to improve their grades, and to use the experience of imagery to open their imaginations. I also hoped they might get an awareness of their senses, a good self-concept and learn to believe that they are creative. Too many here just don't believe it, but they do have good imaginations!

I think that children use imagery all during the day. *They* may have known it, but *we* surely didn't realize it! So now I ask them, 'How many of you play cops and robbers? Play in the doll house?' They say 'Oh, I do!' 'That's imagery,' I say. 'You are using it.' Now I realize that I've always been really good at imagery, but I just didn't realize it! Sometimes I don't see anything, no visual images, but I feel the images like a presence. I guess that is kinesthetic imagery. That is something I've learned: imagery involves all the intelligences, every one."

KAREN

"I'd been having lots of problems. I couldn't get my kids (they're motor disabled) to relax. They have such poor concentration skills that nothing seemed to work.

I like imagery. I thought it was just hypnosis when I started this project. That is what I was taught in college. But now I believe it's using your imagination to learn. Imagery is lots of self-awareness: being more aware of what I think and how I think and what I can do to change it.

It is good having no limitations on how I use imagery. I feel like I can try to find out which way is right for me. At first it was like digging a hole and not knowing where it was going. Now, it is more of an adventure with my children.

They do have good imaginations. Rather than sit still and do quiet imagery exercises though,I've been trying to let all my students do what I call 'moving imagery.' Like, my eight year old, she just can't relax! So while I was trying to teach her to drop and catch a ball, I said 'Just imagine it as a yo-yo.' That worked a little bit. So when I was working with the little boy (I hate to be still with him at all because he needs to learn how to move less awkwardly) I had him put on 'magic shoes' that would help him balance as he walked along. It is working. At least I'm more encouraged now. They've taught me about imagery, too. Or, they taught me to notice it. I noticed one boy instructing himself with imagery! He said repeatedly, 'My beanbag is going through the hole.'

And then he'd throw it. Over and over, he did that. I thought it was so great because he said that. It's just the way he thinks!

There was really no doubt how I would use imagery. I wanted to lose weight! I wanted to improve the ways I deal with my daughter. Especially, I needed something new, a new way to teach these kids. They needed more motor control and they really needed a self-concept boost. It was a big order. It still is, but it does seem to be working."

LISA continues talking about how she used imagery:

"The focus of my work with imagery became clear because of something my husband did. He was telling our daughter a story about when he was a little boy on a hunting trip. I'd heard stories about Mark before, but I'd never heard that one! Maybe I hadn't listened, because when he was telling Georgia about hunting, an image came to me like an explosion: he loves to hunt, which was really driving me crazy, because he loves the quiet and peacefulness of the woods. *That* made sense! I think I'm a lot more empathetic now.

So, through this experience, I decided I wanted to work with images in my family. I know it is easier for me to remember what happened in my childhood than to recall what happened this morning. I decided to use that ability to work with social and emotional issues. I think when you feel the feelings you had as a child, you see how much what I call 'spirit-squashing' went on. I realize how very important it is to keep in touch with feelings, no matter what they are. I'm especially interested in how imagery can help children identify and share feelings with each other."

KATHY

"I began using imagery personally. We needed a new rug and I tried to image it in the space where it would go. My husband measured the space, but I imaged it correctly. It didn't take me long to realize how important imagery could be in classroom use. I really wanted to help my children. More importantly, I wanted to empower them to help themselves. In my first few experiences with imagery, I recognized its possibilities to empower people. I knew it could work with my children, too. I wanted to find a way to work it into the existing curriculum and to make it a part of my students' natural repertoire. It's working! I wish I'd known this years ago!"

KAREN responds, telling about changes that occurred due to imagery practice:

"The kids are learning to concentrate by using imagery! They've learned to concentrate on hitting the target rather than just wildly throwing the ball. One child, David, was scoring close to zero hits until he began to concentrate on the target, on hitting the white wall behind the target. There was an immediate response! He began hitting eight out of ten! It was just phenomenal improvement!

The first child on our videotape showed great improvement too, between 50 and 90% each time. He's doing really well, Billy. He's LD

(learning disabled) and was not learning his alphabet and things like that. I think imagery is really helping him to think of the letters in a different way. He's so imaginative and creative. This LD label could affect him for the rest of his life unless we pay attention to his imagistic ways of thinking and how they relate to his learning! Chances are he'll learn his alphabet, and more, unless, as Lisa said, we 'spirit squash' him.

Margaret showed remarkable improvement on the videotape, too. When I had asked her to jump a rope, she could jump only once, if then, without missing. So I guided her in images of herself jumping the rope perfectly. On the tape you can see this, but Margaret closed her eyes tightly and squeezed her hands into fists. She leaned her body forward into a half-crouched position as she imaged. Then she seemed satisfied and tried again. She jumped five times before she missed! I really think she missed then because she got so excited over her success! It was great!

They are all getting interested in learning things. That is why I'm excited about teaching again. Before this, learning was the last thing they wanted. I think we're getting to the point where they do care. Learning is becoming more a part of them.

I guess it all works together, but they seem to be feeling better about themselves, too. Because they are different in how they move, other kids pick on them, and that is painful. In spite of that, they seem more confident and even more courageous now because of this imagery practice. Someone told me that self-image is nothing more than the image we have of ourselves. Maybe they've changed the images they had. I believe they have.

Mostly, I was really surprised at how much imagery changed me! I guess I thought I was just working with the kids, but it affected me most of all. I used to think that working with these children was limiting. Now I know it isn't, it's just different. I've learned to use imagery to see the good things I do and not just when I'm completely ineffective. In terms of the whole imagery project, it was my personal gains that were the most important. It was more important than the work I did with my kids because, before this, I was so limited in being able to help them."

LISA

"Images help the kids. I don't think there is any doubt they are thinking in images. For instance, the other night, Georgia told her Daddy to close his eyes and make a picture on his mind. He did and then he told her a story, which was a little bit scary as it was Halloween. Georgia said, 'Daddy, I will just scrape that picture off my mind!' This morning, she told me that she had been sad, 'but my sad ran into the ground just like the water from the hose.' Images! I really enjoy listening for them now.

You (Lane Waas) asked her what the 'black' was like, after she told me she sometimes only saw black when she tried to make images. You were right! She wasn't afraid of seeing black. That was just an adult idea, I guess. She made this drawing for me to give to you. It's of her, the little figure in pink. All of the scribbling is 'the black'. I wrote her words on it because she asked me to tell you, 'It's me inside that black. I look all scribbly-scrabbly, but we would feel warm inside that black.'

I am just thinking more about imagery. I thought about LD kids and how much trouble they have learning to spell. Well, if imagery trains visual memory, would it help kids to spell? I keep thinking of ways I want to try to use imagery when I get back in the classroom.

I personally have two kinds of imagery. One of them just pops up from within and the other, which I call 'synthesized imagery', I conjure up. Funny images work best to help me remember things, like my image of a boxer with bright red gloves that punches the air when I'm really angry.

Guess what I did to quit smoking? I smoked in front of the mirror, just to see whatever came across my mind. I thought 'It's just like blowing bubbles!' I wondered if I wanted to smoke really badly, maybe I could just blow bubbles to relieve something in me, to kick the habit! So, I may be going around town blowing bubbles. That's going to be my substitute!"

"It's me inside
that black.
 I look all
scribbly-scrabbly,
but we would
feel warm inside
that black."

Georgia 11-7-86

KATHY concludes...

"My children's grades, especially in science, have skyrocketed! I believe it is because of the relaxation imagery we do. They just keep improving. This last time I had no F's! I had two students who made C's and the rest were 100's! I've kept a chart to show their improvement following imagery exercises over several weeks time (see page 14 for chart). So now they are feeling better about themselves because they are doing better in science. It is clear their self-images are better now!

Also, I don't have the regular arguments going on! We've really become a little community from imagery practice. What we have here now is our little family.

Imagery is a part of their personal repertoire now. They are aware that they are using imagery and that they can use it anytime they want to. Annie's mother called me to say how excited she is over her daughter's changes. Annie's real quiet, so sometimes I can't tell exactly what she's feeling. But her Mom said she loves the imagery, that it makes her feel really secure. She asked me please to continue using it. I told her I plan to do that, every year that I teach!

So, I can say that it helps my children to focus on tasks, it helps them to feel secure, to be more original and creative. It helped them to work better and to improve their grades. They are more in touch with themselves, especially their senses. One child wrote after imagery, 'I can taste the lemon now, like when I'm dreaming.'

I've always enjoyed teaching but, since I've been involved with imagery, I am more creative and I look forward to the next day at work!"

IMAGINATION AND LEARNING:
EXERCISES

Imagination reveals itself in the balance or reconciliation of opposite qualities...the idea with the image.   Samuel Taylor Coleridge

Begin by looking for a few seconds at a candle flame. Close your eyes and look at the bright after-images. Now see this ball of light you are looking at behind your closed eyes turn into a sunflower with bright yellow petals, a brown seeded center, and a long green stalk. Move closer to the sunflower. Now dive through the center, feeling the rough seeds fall away as you swim through them. Enter now into the heart of the sunflower and find there a golden sun. Swim amidst the bright gases of the sun for a while. Feel the heat all over your body. Now dive deeper into the sun until you find a sunflower. Take one of its seeds and eat it, wishing yourself home. The seed has magic powers, for you open your eyes and find yourself back.   Dr. Jean Houston

Introduction to Imagery Exercises

It may sometimes seem difficult in teaching and parenting to change one's methods and processes. Working with imagery is not so much a change as it is a bonus to parenting, teaching and learning. As you begin to venture into your own thinking processes, your own mind, you can discover strengths and skills there that are creative and strong.

In sections of this book, I have pointed out the necessity for getting on with the exciting business of encouraging and teaching our children to fully use their natural imagistic abilities. We, as parents and teachers must relearn and practice what we have forgotten and begin to be aware of and use our own imagistic intelligences.

Barbara Clark[1], in her ground-breaking book, Optimizing Learning, states clearly that only if parents and educators "...are willing to create, explore, grow and learn will they succeed in bringing the opportunity for excellence into the...lives of all children." Educators must work together with parents to see that these potentials are developed and actualized. They can begin by learning exactly what conditions must be established, and what processes can be used for themselves, in order to guide the children in their care.

Steps for Guiding Imagery Exercises

> Although imagery appears to be wired into the human organism...certain conditions appear to be necessary for it to emerge. Still others help it to flourish.[2]

There are six steps for guiding imagery exercises. At first, it is important to be certain that each step is included. Many teachers who practice imagery regularly find that within a short time the steps fall into place naturally and they no longer have to keep count.

Beverly Galyean first defined these steps in her pioneering imagery work in California schools during the 1970's.

1. Relaxation/Centering:
Settle and clear the mind of distractions.

2. Focusing:
Sharpen inner perception and aid image control.

3. Multisensing:
Involve a maximum number of process mechanisms.

4. Imaging:
Use visual, auditory, kinesthetic, olfactory, gustatory and/or any other of the senses. (A recent publication listed more than 100!)

5. Expression:
Communicate, using means such as writing, drawing, singing and/or other expressive modes.

6. Reflection/Interpretation:
Receive personal and group feedback. This process aids group-building.

Galyean has suggested that beginning steps be simple ones which lead to the longer and more complex journeys into imagery within which practitioners may go "to various places," be involved "in new situations," and come in "contact with different people and objects."

I became familiar with Howard Gardner's work primarily through his books relating to art. During my three-year training program at the Foundation for Brain and Mind Research, I attended a conference in Tarrytown, N.Y. during which he presented his theory of multiple intelligences[3]. Since then, I have been convinced that a major road to quality educational practice lies through the development of ways to implement his theory.

Talents, skills, potentials, know-how, gifts, intelligences: I have discovered that each person has access to one or more of these. When empowered, they help to form the coherent sense of self necessary for confident and quality learning.

What follows is a listing of the seven intelligences and their characteristics (quoted from The Educational Researcher, November, 1989, "Multiple Intelligences Go to School," by Howard Gardner and Thomas Hatch). We've added symbol images for each intelligence.

THE SEVEN INTELLIGENCES

✛ **Logical-Mathematical:** Sensitivity to, and capacity to discern, logical or numerical patterns and the ability to handle long chains of reasoning.

👄 **Verbal-Linguistic:** Sensitivity to the sounds, rhythms and meanings of words as well as a sensitivity to the different functions of language.

𝄞 **Musical:** Abilities to produce and appreciate rhythm, pitch and timbre with an appreciation of the many forms of musical expressiveness.

👁 **Visual-Spatial:** Capacities to perceive the visual-spatial world accurately and to perform transformations on one's initial perceptions.

🏃 **Bodily-Kinesthetic:** Abilities to control one's body movements and to handle objects skillfully.

👥 **Interpersonal:** Capacities to discern and respond appropriately to the moods, temperaments, motivations and desires of other people.

🧘 **Intrapersonal:** Access to one's own feelings as well as the ability to discriminate among them and draw upon them to guide behavior plus the knowledge of one's own strengths, weaknesses, desires and intelligences.

Gardner postulates that

"...It is possible that the intelligences can function both as subject matters in themselves and as the preferred means for inculcating diverse subject matter...For every goal currently being pursued, there is...a set of intelligences which could readily be mobilized for its realization..."

Following, I have written imagery exercises for a variety of developmental abilities and age groups, from early childhood through adulthood. As you experience each of them, you can understand how they integrate subjects, pertain to several areas of development and involve several intelligences. You also may notice how, with slight variation, they may be used for either adults or children. I have designed them individually to meet an educational or life goal, reinforce one or more of Gardner's intelligences, demonstrate imagery use in mental, physical, emotional and spiritual applications and to **be enjoyable!**

Index of Imagery Exercises

I have indexed the imagery exercises according to the intelligence or intelligences that they address. I hope this listing will be helpful by making the exercises easy to locate and by letting you see several ways that the intelligences may interrelate in their imaginative forms. These exercises have been used by students and teachers alike in a variety of ways and for diverse purposes. The main purpose of these exercises is to develop each person's strengths and gifts.

A RELAXATION EXERCISE

✠ LOGICAL-MATHEMATICAL INTELLIGENCE: EXERCISES

BODILY-KINESTHETIC INTELLIGENCE: EXERCISES

INTERPERSONAL INTELLIGENCE: EXERCISES

INTRAPERSONAL INTELLIGENCE: EXERCISES

Imagery Exercises

Beginning exercises can be as simple as the suggestion to close your eyes and focus on a colored shape, perhaps a red circle. Next, you could change the color, perhaps several times. You could also change the *shape*, perhaps to a square and then change the size of the square. You could then change the shapes into objects, such as buildings, trucks, or beach balls.

Next, involve other senses by imagining what a green circle smells like, how a black square feels or what sound a red circle makes. Then ask which shape or which color tastes best? This multisensory approach creates more "hooks and eyes" which anchor images, and it allows access and opportunity to all styles of learning.

When this practice has been successfully experienced, you are ready to begin to use the longer imagery exercises. Very young children and some older ones, will continue to profit from using brief exercises.

The following exercises are examples of a variety of types of imagery use. They range from cognitive exercises to affective exercises to psychophysical exercises. [See Bloom, 1956, or Galyean, 1983, for expanded explanations of these "domains" of learning.] I have also included exercises to develop intuition. Quoting Frances Vaughn once again, "Imagery is the language of intuition" and leads to the development of that important and often neglected perception.

I recommend several additional exercises from sources listed at the end of this book. I studied with Dr. Jean Houston at the Foundation for Brain and Mind Research and experienced her exercises as profound. Simpler ones and those more appropriate for children, may be found in the other listed books. Dr. Tom Roberts was my mentor at the beginning of my imagery studies and I think his book (co-authored with Dr. Gay Hendricks) is superb. Dr. Roberts' work focuses upon consciousness studies, of which imagery is an integral part.

I hope that you will emerge from the reading of this book and the practice of these exercises, with an understanding that will enable you to design imagery exercises to fit your needs. Enjoy your imaging!

General Directions for Using these Imagery Exercises

The language used in imagery exercises is designed to flow. Sharp starts and stops break an imagizer's ability to focus and so they are not as effective. As you read the exercises, allow the words and phrases to blend and stream together. They may be read aloud as they are written. Ellipsis marks in the exercises indicate that a silent waiting period should occur to give the imagizer sufficient time to create his or her images.

A Relaxation Exercise

Use this as a beginning for *any* imagery exercise. It is also effective by itself for relaxation and stress reduction. Regular practice of this exercise can lead toward the development of a personal stress management program. It should be done very slowly, with time between the statements for all participants to complete their imagery. In its full length, it is best suited for older children and adults. It can easily be shortened for very young children.

Allow your body to find a comfortable position...sitting, or lying down, if possible. Allow your eyes to relax...to close gently. As you breathe, take slow, deep breaths and let the breaths begin to relax you. Breathe in fresh, clean air...breathe out fatigue and stress. Breathing all the way in...noticing your breath...and breathing all the way out, follow your breathing with your awareness of it. In...and out...Continue now breathing in...and out...and in...and out...and in...and out. Continue this breathing for about one minute on your own while I am silent. As you do so, feel your body as it relaxes. Realize that your mind, too, is relaxing, while it is also remaining alert. You are relaxed...and alert. Breathe in...and

out...[One minute]. **Good. Now, notice your feet and toes. Stretch them a little...and then let them relax...Rotate your ankles...and relax them. Tense the muscles in your calves just a bit...and then turn them loose...let them relax. Also tense the muscles in your thighs...and let them completely relax. Squeeze your buttocks...and relax...Relax your stomach...and your lower back...Tense your shoulders by raising them a little...and then relax them, and your whole upper back. Just let them sink into the floor. [Or say, ..."sink** like warm honey," if imagers are sitting up.] **Breathe deeply again, and as you exhale, let your upper abdomen and chest relax...letting all tension go...Relax your upper arms....and your lower arms...Make a fist with each of your hands....and turn them loose. Feel your fingers relaxing. Moving up your arms to your shoulders, check to**

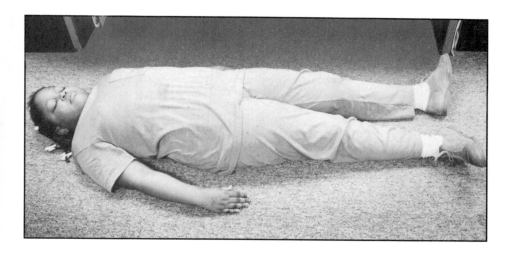

see if they are still relaxed...just completely relaxed. Now relax your neck...and the whole back of your head...and your crown...and your forehead...Just let all the tension slide off your forehead, as you completely relax your face... Relax your eyes... letting them sink comfortably into their sockets...Relax your nose...Relax your mouth...Open it wide, and then let it relax. Relax your tongue and your jaw...letting your mouth remain slightly open. Now, for a moment, feel your whole body as it is completely relaxed. Continue gently breathing now...as we move into guided imagery...[Or, when this exercise is used alone, counting can be used to restore complete alertness to participants. For example, *"Continue breathing now. As I count from ten to one, please join me at the count of six. When we reach one, clap your hands and find yourself wide awake, alert and very relaxed. Beginning now, 10...9...8..."*]

Many of the following exercises are for young children, yet they may be expanded for use with older students by using more complex ideas than these illustrated. Be sure to maintain harmony between the active feeling, sensing and doing processes and the cognitive concepts.

Mathematics for Children   ☦

Cognitive imagery, this exercise addresses the Logical-Mathmatical Intelligence, as defined by Howard Gardner in <u>Frames of Mind</u>.

Children, I am drawing on the board the number five: 5. See it? Beneath it, I am drawing the number two: 2. Here is the addition sign: +. I will draw a line beneath it all, and we can add the numbers together. What is the answer? Seven: 7? Yes. Good. Look at it very carefully. Can you see it well? Good. Now, I want you to close your eyes...right. Everyone let your eyes close. Just as we have done before, take a deep, slow breath...and let it out. Do it

again...breathe...and let it out...Again, breathe...let it out. Good. Now, I want you to imagine that you can see on a movie screen on the back of your eyelids a large number 5. See it there? Make it whichever color you choose. Good. Now, beneath the five, see a large number 2. Color it also. Is it there now? Can you see the big colorful 2 beneath the 5? Good. Now, see the addition sign in front of the 2...and the line beneath it. Then see the answer in the brightest color you know. Can you see it? Seven: 7? Good. Now open your eyes and see if your pictures or images of the numbers look like the ones I wrote on the board. Do they? Except yours are more colorful? Right! Close your eyes once more and see them again. I'll wait while you see them...And open your eyes and compare them again...Yours are prettier, eh? Yes, I'll have to use colored chalk next time! Very good. You did that very well. Let's take crayons now and draw those colorful numbers on your papers. Do that now...[allow adequate time]. How pretty they look! What fine numbers you are writing! (When completed:) What do you like best about your number-drawings? Was that fun to do? Good. Thank you.

Quiet and Noisy

Designed to develop Listening Skills with young children, this exercise addresses the Verbal-Linguistic Intelligence as defined by Gardner.

Now let's make some images of quiet things. Close your eyes and breathe deeply. Can I hear you breathing? Yes...good. Now, I will name some quiet things and I would like you to do your best to imagine these things just as clearly as you can. Imagine how quiet they are. Okay? Now...imagine a whisper...a very quiet whisper...Imagine soft rain falling in the grass. Imagine yourself tiptoeing barefoot across a very soft rug. Imagine the quiet sounds you hear when you first wake up in the morning...or from naptime...Imagine someone humming a pretty song. Imagine listening to a story. Good. These are all quiet sounds, aren't they? Open your eyes now and tell me something about the sounds or the images that you experienced. [Allow adequate time for all, especially the quiet or shy child who may be slower to share, but who wishes to do so]. Good. Now you may take the crayons and paper and draw pictures of some quiet things.

Now let's make some images of noisy things. Do we sometimes like noisy things? Are *we* sometimes noisy things? Yes...well, let's imagine some others now. Close your eyes and breathe deeply. Can I hear you breathing? Can you hear the whole group breathing? Yes, that is not a very noisy thing, though, is it? I will name some noisy things and I would like you to do your best to imagine these things just as clearly as you can. Imagine how noisy they are. OK? Now...imagine the telephone ringing...Imagine our whole group outside playing and laughing...Imagine the sound of thunder...Imagine running and talking with your pet, or with your best friend...Imagine the sound of an airplane, a jet plane...Imagine your blocks crashing down into a big pile...Imagine someone creeping up behind you and teasing you by shouting "BOO!" Oh...that *is* very noisy, isn't it! Sometimes things that are close to us sound very noisy, don't they? Open your eyes now and let's talk about the noisy images you experienced. (Allow adequate time.) **Now, you may draw a picture of noisy things, using the crayons and paper** (or paint or whatever art supplies are available).

Discussion can include the appropriateness of quietness and noisiness in various places and times. It would be helpful to point out the differences in the pictures. If there is space, hang them. Ask the children to notice the color differences, the shape differences, etc. The noisier pictures will often be more vivid or darker in color as well as more angular. Textures and directions of lines may also differ. Notice this non-verbal way of communicating information. These similarities and differences are the basis for understanding art.

Treasure Hunt

An exercise in visual memory skills for young children, this exercise addresses the Visual-Spatial Intelligence as defined by Gardner.

Today we are going to take an imaginary trip. We will imagine ourselves walking quietly around the room looking for some objects as I suggest them. For instance, if I ask you to imagine where I am sitting, can you do that with your eyes closed? Yes, of course you can. Good. So, let's begin by closing our eyes and breathing deeply. Breathing deeply relaxes us so that we can think clearly...Can I hear you breathing?...Good. Now, I would like for you to imagine, without peeking, where the door to the hallway is located...Without opening your eyes, raise your hand and point to the doorway... Good. Now, imagine seeing where the clock is located...and point to it... Good. Where did you hang your jacket or your sweater today?...Where are the blocks located?...Where is our choice board?...Where is our art center?...Good. Now, where is your favorite spot in the room?...Imagine all that you can see there...Point to it. Oh, good. Now, let's open our eyes and go right to the crayons and draw all the things you saw in your favorite spot in the room.

A variation on this exercise is to review Putting Things Away. Several items can be strung together in imagery so long as the child's attention span is considered.

Putting Things Away

This exercise also pertains to visual memory skills for young children. It addresses the Visual-Spatial Intelligence.

Now it is time to put things away so that we may get ready to go home for the day. Let's take another imaginary trip and, as you sit where you are now and close your eyes, imagine those things with which you are playing. See them again...with your eyes closed. Now, see them magically flying back into their own storage places. Can you see them there? Where do they go?...Just quietly think where they go...Can you see them on the shelves, or in the cupboard, or in the boxes, or wherever they belong? Are they placed so they can rest there until we come here again tomorrow? Good. Now, when I finish telling you this...but not until I finish telling you...open your eyes and, without rushing, take those things and put them into the places that you have imagined them...When you have finished, come and sit in the circle so that I will know you are finished...Now, open your eyes and do that...

Now that we are all sitting in our circle, let's look around the room and see all our things in the places where they belong, in their resting places. We'll enjoy coming into this pretty room tomorrow

to begin another day together. Do you ever imagine where your things at home belong? Do you put them away like we did here today? Good. That is something to be proud of and I am proud of *you*. Aren't you proud of yourself, too? If you would like to draw while you are at home, draw a picture of some of your things exactly in the places where they belong. If you do, please bring your drawings with you tomorrow so that we can all see them. Thank you.

Self-Image

An affective imagery exercise, designed as an art activity for young children, addresses the Intrapersonal Intelligence.

Let's begin today by lying down on the floor and being very still. Good. Now begin to breathe deeply and slowly...I want to hear you breathing. Good. Notice your breathing...how it makes your chest rise as you breathe in...and fall as you breathe out...Try it again...slowly now. Breathing in...and out...Good. Today our imagery exercise is about us! We will imagine us! We'll imagine a

portrait of us. A portrait is a painting of ourselves. So, begin by imagining a portrait of yourself: your head...your body...chest, tummy, back, hips, buttocks...and your legs...and your feet...and your arms... and your hands...your hair... ears...eyes and eyebrows. Good. Now, what are you wearing?...What kind of clothes would you like to be wearing in your portrait?...What kind of shoes? Are they tie-shoes? Buckle shoes? How do they fasten?...What color are your clothes and shoes?...Do you have on any rings? Or other jewelry?...*Where* would you like to be in your portrait?...At school? At home? Somewhere else?...What things will be around you in your portrait?...Can you see this portrait as a big one? Maybe as big as you are? Or even bigger?...Now see it small...maybe as big as your tablet...Does that make a difference?...Let it become large again...as large as the big pieces of kraft paper you saw on the table. See your portrait as clearly as you can...Notice all its details...and, when you are ready, quietly get up (so you don't disturb anyone who isn't ready yet) and find a place at the table and begin to paint the portrait that you imagined today. You may close your eyes to look at it again anytime you wish.

I find that children, as well as adults, can image across time limits. They can successfully observe historical occurances, such as the Pilgrims arriving at Plymouth Rock or the way their lives might have been if their ancestors had been their parents or friends. They can imagine present-day events, such as the hunting trip exercise outlined later, or teaching someone else how to do imagery. Future imaginings, such as what the music of the future will sound like, also occur in imagery. What will cars look like? What new ways can be imagined to clean up the environment? Most people know and can imagine much more than they first believe they can.

One Hundred Years Ago

By tying what we know to what we imagine and so engaging creative thinking, this exercise addresses the Bodily-Kinesthetic, Visual-Spatial, Logical-Mathematical, Personal and Linguistic Intelligences.

Today we will take a Time Adventure! We will imagine that we are living one hundred years ago and that those people who are our great-great-grandparents, who probably none of us knew, are our best friends. Let us begin by sitting very quietly...very straight...and let our eyes close. As we breathe deeply...as we all breathe together...I can hear you breathing slowly and deeply. Let us imagine that there stretches out behind us a time line. It can be just like the one that we are using in social studies, only without any

dates or any events on it. Imagine the long line...stretching out behind us. As we continue to breathe, we can see that line very clearly, and we know that it will lead us on a Time Adventure today. It is also the line that will bring us back to this day and this room when we finish our adventure. So, in our imaginations, let's slowly turn around and face that line, which has been stretching out behind us. Good. Now, that line stretches out for as far as we can see, or even imagine. We know, because we have planned it that way, that this line will take us back one hundred years...to a different kind of school from this one...to a different kind of house...and a different family and different friends. But it *really* is our family because they are our ancestors: those people who were our great-great-grandparents.

As we begin walking down the Line that is taking us to the time one hundred years ago, we first notice things only a few years back, perhaps five or ten. Do we see anything that is different? Have the recycling bins not been invented yet? Are the toys that we see lying about in yards different from the ones we have in our current time? What else is different?...Can we see how people probably really liked these differences?...Can we enjoy them, too?

Moving further back into time, about twenty-five or thirty years, your parents were children...What have they told you about their childhood that you can see now, as we pass through their time? Why are older students angry? What are they protesting?... Have you ever heard of President Kennedy? He is president in this time of the early nineteen sixties...Do you know about Martin Luther King Jr.? Can you see him leading a peaceful march with many people following him?...What do the automobiles look like?...Where are the places to eat, like Burger King? Wendys? Taco Bell?...What is Viet Nam? Why are our soldiers there?...

Moving on down the Line, now it is fifty years ago, the nineteen forties. Another war is just ending. Many uniforms, flags, injured soldiers...many happy soldiers coming home to waiting families again...We, at home, can buy gasoline, sugar, candy bars, and nylon stockings again. What was it like without them?...Why is milk in glass bottles?...Toys seem made of metal and of wood...where is plastic?...Your grandparents are children in this time. What can you ask them to tell you about living in the time of fifty years ago?... Ask them to tell you about the Depression...about how it was to have no money, about how people traded or bartered goods and services...how people paid the local doctor in chickens and vegetables. Ask them now...in your imagination...and moving on...

Seventy-five years ago...your great-grandparents are children now. Look. They are riding about in buggies and on horseback and in wagons. They are walking...It seems a long way to walk to school on dirt roads. Schools are small, often just one room. All the children gather there and study together. What is that like?...Many people are working on farms. The children do not go to school when there are fields to be worked or crops to be harvested...Do you like that?... Do you like harvesting the crops?...Ask your great-grandparents to tell you about harvesting the crops...about how all the children have important tasks to do to keep the farms running...Does your great-grandmother cook for the whole family, even as a young girl? How many were there in her family? Eight? Ten? Twelve? What does she think of our small families in current time?...Do your great-grandparents even dream of radio?...or of television?...of stereo?... telephones or even electricity?...of going to the movies?...of a place like Disney World?...MacDonalds?...What were their toys? Do the girls help to make their dolls?...Do the boys make toys, too?...Ask them what it is like to be a child in their day...

Walking on to the end of today's Time Line, it is now 100 years ago. Our great-great grandparents are children and as we find ourselves in their time, they come up and speak to us...befriend us...They ask if we'd like to come to their houses to visit. We say "Yes, we really would like that," because that is why we came on this adventure today. Take a few minutes to walk with your new friends...to ask them questions...to listen to their stories about their lives...to notice all that you can possibly see...and smell...and hear...and touch...

When you arrive home with them, and find dinner ready, notice what the meal tastes like...what it looks like...How is it different from what you would have if you were back in your home?...Play with your new friends...Ask them to teach you one of their games...Ask if you may teach them one of your favorites...Are they alike? Similar?

Thank them for such a wonderful time...You notice that it is now time to begin the walk upon the Time Line back to your own time. But look! They have offered you a gift to take with you...Perhaps you have brought something in your pocket that you might want to leave with them...Thanking them again, turn and begin the walk back up the Time Line to your time...passing the time of seventy-five years ago...and fifty years ago...speaking and waving as you pass...thirty years ago...ten years ago...and walking straight back into *this* Time and *this* room now. Stretch a bit. Stand up and stretch...and now, take your papers and write a story about your favorite time on your Time Adventure. Write about as many things as you can recall... your...friends...your ancestor...houses...schools...toys ...and so on. Enjoy the story as you write it.

When you finish, use pencils or crayons or paints to represent the gift you were given and the friends who gave it to you. Let's call these "Portraits from the Past."

Make More Sense

This exercise may be a science or social-studies exercise. It addresses the Kinesthetic, Visual-Spatial, and Verbal-Linguistic Intelligences and the sense of smell. I have adapted it from an exercise for adults taught me by Dr. Jean Houston.

As you remember, we have been learning about our senses. Today we are going to take an imaginary journey to learn more about our sense of smell. So, to begin...as we always begin this way...just start to relax. Get comfortable by sitting straight in your desk. [Or, if possible, lie flat on the floor.] Put both feet flat on the floor. This helps the oxygen you breathe to get to every part of your body...Breathe now...and notice that what you are breathing has a smell...Take a big breath...in...and let it out slowly...In...and out...In...and out...Good. Now let's imagine we are walking down the street...a lovely street...a different street from the one we usually walk...and we see a beautiful old house. We decide to go in because there is a

"WELCOME" sign on the door and our teacher says she has been here before. It is okay for us to go inside. As we enter, we see a great big room...and in it are all kinds of things to smell...good smells...and not-so-good smells. We decide to clean it up and throw out the bad-smelling things, so we gather big trashbags and, like good citizens, we begin...We see and smell old leftover hamburgers in their torn wrappers...someone's dog's food bowl...wet sneakers...ICKY!...let's throw them all out. Are there any others?... Gather them, too...Now isn't it nicer? What are the good smells you notice?... Let's open the window and let the fresh air blow into the room...Do you smell flowers?... Someone is cooking a good lunch...What is it?... Do you smell the cookies?... Ah, there are fresh soapy suds to wash our hands...What else do you smell that smells good to you?...

Okay...Now it is time to go back into the classroom, so let's gather up the bags of smelly junk that we've tied tightly and we'll put them into the receptacles outside. The old bits of food we have gathered go into the compost pile. We can recycle most of the rest of it! There are containers for plastics, for glass, for paper and for beverage cans. This is a very good way to help our environment too...What a lovely smelling place it is now!...We can return here anytime, just by imagining. Let's be in our classroom again now...Was that fun? What are some of your favorite things to smell? Were they in your imaginary room? Let's write a story today about the smells in the big old house. You may write it with crayons if you wish. When we all finish, you may read yours to the class if you would like...

It is easy to imagine how the various senses could be used in imagery exercises to complement this one. Trips into the big old house could be used for visual, auditory, tactile or gustatory learning. In today's world we continue to identify various other "senses." This kind of exercise can be expanded to include all of the senses while fostering an awareness of ways to clean up the environment.

Sharing Caring: Relationships

Addressing the Personal Intelligences as well as Verbal-Linguistic, Bodily-Kinesthetic and Visual-Spatial Intelligences, this exercise can be used as a Social Studies or Communications Skills lesson. It is designed to follow an on-going study and discussion of feelings. To begin a study, you may prefer to change some of the wording.

We have been talking a lot about feelings lately. What kinds of feelings can you think of ?...Good. Are there any others?...Okay. Today, I've planned an imagery exercise where we can give each other good feelings. When we *give* good feelings, we get them for ourselves! What are some good feelings? Happiness...Fun... Love... Caring...Looking forward to something...Seeing something pretty... Good. These are fine examples. Are there any others?... Okay.

Please stand up today...by your same partner from this morning's exercise. Stand beside your partner...and listen carefully. I will tell you what the exercise is about...Good. Let's start with the good feeling we call "caring." This partner is your friend, and we all care about our friends, don't we? So, let's begin this exercise by sitting down...on the floor...facing your partner. Yes, get close enough almost to touch knees...and let your eyes close...Begin to breathe deeply now...and easily...and breathe in...and out...in...and

out...in...and out...Good. We are relaxing our bodies as we breathe...in...and out...Good. Now, just imagine the good feeling of "caring"...Can you feel what "caring" feels like to you?... Can you locate it in your feelings?...In your body?...Is it in your tummy?... or your chest?...or your head?...Where is it? Just imagine where your caring is...What does it look like?...Is it a color?...And now that you have found it, take it in your imaginary hands and give it to your partner...Just imagining...imagine that you are doing that now...Good. Now, for a minute, just know how it feels to receive caring from your partner...You are just receiving caring now...What is that like for you?...Now give some more caring to your partner...and receive some more caring from your partner...Very good. Now, take a deep breath and notice your toes and wiggle them a bit...And wiggle your fingers...As you open your eyes now...stretch a little bit...Very good. Okay. Seat yourself in your chairs now and let's talk about what it was like sharing "caring" with your friend...

Frances Vaughn called imagery "the language of intuition." Intuition seems to reveal itself throughout the "intelligences." In this exercise, we explore intuition to become more aware of its role in the thinking process and to notice the profound effects of this kind of thinking.

Learning About Intuition

Affective imagery for a wider age range, this addresses all the intelligences, but particularly the Intrapersonal Intelligence. It can be used as a creative writing lesson, an art lesson, or used in any discipline where self-awareness and intuition are important.

Intuition is a way of knowing that is different from our regular way of knowing. Do you ever get a hunch about something? What?... Yes...that is intuition. We're going to do an exercise about intuition today. We're going to let intuitive images come into our imagination and notice what they are. Whatever those images are is absolutely okay. We won't try to invent them and we won't change them. We'll just do our best to *notice* them. Okay?

Sit quietly now, and begin to relax...just letting your whole body relax...Let your feet relax...and your legs...Let your buttocks and your back relax...and your tummy...your chest...your neck and your eyes...your mouth and even your tongue can relax...Good.

Now, imagine that when you woke up this morning, you discovered that for today you could be a wonderful animal...Look at yourself...What animal are you?...How does it feel to be that animal?...Imagine that you find a magic wand as you are walking around as an animal, and when you nuzzle it... (Wouldn't you do that if you were an animal?) you become a beautiful flower, or tree! Which are you?...a flower?...a tree?...What kind of flower or tree are you? ...What do you like about being that particular flower, or tree? ...Next, you become a geometric shape...What shape are you? Do you like being that shape?...Are you a color? Do you have a texture?...

The last thing you can become on this magic day is a baby...Look at yourself as a baby...Listen to the sounds you make as a baby...Since you are watching this baby now, just lean over and give this baby a gentle hug...a good hug...Feel how it feels to be this baby... Remember now what your images are of being an animal...a flower...a tree...a geometric shape...and a tiny baby...Remember your images of all of these things...

Begin to stretch and notice your relaxed body again...Take a deep breath...and come back into this classroom and find yourself sitting right where we began this imaginary journey...What was that like? Would you like to draw yourself as one of those images? You may draw them now...or, if you prefer, you may write about your experiences...

I have adapted the following exercise from one developed by Karen, a teacher in my study, as she worked with motor disabled students.

Bean Bags

Designed to develop psychomotor skills, this exercise predominantly addresses the Bodily-Kinesthetic Intelligence. Also addressed are Linguistic, Mathematical and Visual-Spatial Intelligences.

You have just thrown bean bags and tried to get them to go through the round hole in the target. Now, in a moment, I want you to *imagine* that you are throwing bean bags through the target. First, let's center ourselves. Do you remember how to do that? Yes...there is a spot just below your navel that is the center of your body...Put your hand over that spot...right...good...Now, close your eyes, and, as you breathe slowly and deeply, pretend that the breath goes into your nose and right down through your body and you catch it in the hand that is over your center spot. Just imagine that you can do that now...breathe in...hold the breath in your hand for a moment...then, let it go and breathe out...Good. Do it again now...breathe in...hold the breath in your hand...breathe out...breathe in...hold it...breathe out. Very good. Now, I want you to imagine that you are throwing bean bags through the target. Feel your imaginary hands pick up the beanbags. Notice how they feel in your hands...Now, imagine that you are seeing the target. You see it very clearly now...The opening seems very large and you are sure that you can hit it with the beanbag. In your imagination, feel yourself throwing the beanbag...Throw it with all your strength...and watch...as the beanbag sails right through the target. BLAM! It hits the wall behind the target...Good. Now, imagine you are picking up another beanbag...You see the large, open target...You are feeling very sure that you can hit it again this time...and you lift your arm and throw the beanbag...BLAM! Right on target! Good. Now, I will wait while you do it again...Did you hit it?...Yes, you did! Good. Do it another time, now...Great! Now, open your eyes, and with your real hands, pick up the real beanbag and throw it through the real, large opening, just as you did it in your imagination...Keep throwing now, until you have thrown five real beanbags. Count as you throw them...1...2...3...4...5! You may stop and image throwing one at any time.

The following three exercises were written by my beginning adult imagery students. They are designed for use with very young children.

Birds

Designed for three-year olds, it addresses the Verbal-Linguistic, Musical, Visual-Spatial, Kinesthetic and Intrapersonal Intelligences. The numbers represent the steps of an imagery exercise.

1. Ask the children to **jump up and down to release excess energy**.

2. Ask the children to **lie down and close their eyes.**

3. Do a deep breathing exercise together. **Listen to your breath...**

4. **Pretend you are standing outside in the yard. Do you see the green grass? the tall trees? the flowers? What colors are they? Red...yellow...white...Yes. Good. Now, do you see the bird? How does it look? The bird seems to be moving. What is it doing? Oh, listen. Do you hear the bird? What sound does it make?**

5. & 6. Ask the children to open their eyes and tell you about the bird they saw in their imaginations. Ask them what sounds it made. Ask them to move about like their bird moved. Ask them to draw their bird with crayons.

Circles in Math

Designed for three-year old children, this exercise addresses the Logical-Mathematical, Verbal-Linguistic, Visual-Spatial and Bodily-Kinesthetic Intelligences.

1. **Get in a very comfortable position, such as lying down, and do some deep and slow breathing to help you get relaxed.**

2. & 3. **Notice how your tummy moves when you breathe.**

4. **Now...everyone close your eyes. Take a very big breath and let it out. Listen to it as it goes out...We have been talking about circles...and we know what a circle looks like...With your eyes closed, imagine that you see a circle. Can you see a big circle? Good. Now, see a small circle. Good. Can you see its color? Now...your circle is very round, isn't it? I want you to turn it into something else that is round...like a cookie, or a beachball, or a wheel, or anything else you can imagine. Be sure it is round like a circle. Good. Now, we have all imagined something that is round like a circle. It is time to come back to our classroom. When I clap my hands we will all be back here in the classroom.**

5. **Stand up now...in our circle...and show me with your hands how big your imaginary circle was. WOW! Big ones...and small ones, too. Good. Now, let's move over to the table and draw the things you imagined. Color them, too, with your crayons. When you have finished, bring them up and we'll hang them right here. Okay?**

6. Later...comment about the drawings. Ask the children to tell about them and write their words beside their drawings.

Melting Process: Science

Addressing the Verbal-Linguistic, Bodily-Kinesthetic, Visual-Spatial and Intrapersonal Intelligences, this is designed for first grade, and includes only Step 4, the imagery portion. The other steps may be substituted from another exercise, or you may want to design your own.

Stand up as we do this imagery exercise. Close your eyes. Have you ever watched something melt? Ice Cream? Ice Cubes? Where does it first start melting? How does it change shape?

You are now a beautiful tall snowman...The sun is shining on your head and you feel very warm...The sun keeps getting warmer and warmer...and the top of your snowman-head starts to melt and

drip. There it goes, dripping down to your shoulders...very relaxed. The sun keeps shining on your shoulders...as they begin to lose their shape and droop, you feel very, very relaxed...Now your body begins to bend over...Let your real body bend now, as your imaginary snowman body bends, too...Your arms and feet and legs begin to feel soft...The sun is warm and comfortable and your shape has changed from a tall snowman into a lovely pool of cool water...Look into the pool and see your real self reflected there...It is time to leave the snowman and the lovely puddle and return to being you, so slowly begin to stand up straight again...stretching your arms, legs, back...I am going to count to ten. Start counting with me when I reach 6, and open your eyes when we reach 10, feeling very good inside and remembering how it feels to be relaxed like a melting snowman...or to feel like a lovely pool of water...and to feel like YOU, as you are now. 1...2...3...4...

Still-Hunting

This observational skills exercise addresses both the Bodily-Kinesthetic and Visual-Spatial Intelligences. It is excellent for use with older children and with adults. My thanks to Dr. Jack Hassard, who introduced me to a similar exercise in his Creativity Workshop.

There is an old Indian legend that tells of how young Indian children were taught to hunt. The first steps are called "Still Hunting." The child was instructed to move very quietly through the woods and find a secluded place upon a hillside from which all the goings-on of the woods could be observed. The object of the hunt was to observe all that could be seen, in great detail. So, the young Indian would find a place to sit quietly, disturbing nothing, and watch, listen and smell all that he could. Today, in this imagery exercise, we will take a similar hunting trip. So...beginning our trip, allow your body to relax while you keep your mind alert. As you do that now...slowly begin to breathe deeply...letting the breath travel to each part of your body...And now, feeling yourself very relaxed, and very alert, we will go on our journey.

Imagine...that you are about to go on a hunting trip, and your main job is to notice everything! Is there anything that you might wish to take with you?...something small and easy to carry?...Take something that will leave no marks and make no sounds, as you will need to be very quiet and still to observe all the wild life...You do not want to frighten anything away...If there is something, gather it now in your image, and bring it with you on the hunt...

Now you find yourself at the edge of the woods...beautiful woods...and the sun is shining and the air is pleasant and warm...You begin to walk into the woods, looking for a place where you can sit quietly and watch everything while not letting yourself be seen. Notice all that you can as you hunt for this special place...Notice the breezes that blow the leaves and change the patterns of light on the forest floor.... Listen to the sounds...of your footsteps...birds...whatever else you may hear...Reach out and touch the bark of a nearby tree, or a flower...Continue through the forest now...noticing all that you can...

Finding your special place now...from where you can watch, move quietly into that place...and sit carefully, trying to disturb as little as possible...If branches have been moved, or insects scattered, wait for a moment for the living things to restore themselves to their natural patterns...For the next three minutes of clock-time, equal to "all the time you will need," and while my voice is silent, pay attention to all that you can, preparing yourself to take with you all the sounds, pictures, feelings, smells, tastes and any other impressions that you can gather during this time. Do that now...[three minutes].

Now, gathering any things that you may have brought with you...and remembering that you may return to this special place whenever you wish...move quietly now...back through the lovely woods...back to the spot where you began this journey...As I count from ten to one, join with me at the count of six. When we reach "one," clap your hands and find yourself wide awake, feeling very refreshed and alert, and remembering all the things that you experienced today. Beginning now...10...9...8...7...6...5...4...3 ...2...1...CLAP.

Take a few minutes now to write about your experiences, or express what you discovered in some way that is meaningful to you. [Other possibilities include improvisational dance, singing, playing musical instruments, drawing, painting, etc...]

There are many opportunities for developing skills through the use of imagery exercises. Research [Endnotes, Research Chapter (1)] shows that many skills increase rapidly when practiced in imagery. Notice that the process of imaging is one in which you image yourself actually doing the skill and not simply watching yourself do it. *Be a part of the action of your images and not simply an onlooker.* These exercises are "kinesthetic body" exercises, (exercises for the muscular imagination.) Skills that require guidance as well as those that evolve from a child's personal exploration and investigation are addressed here. A child can practice putting on and taking off a coat, sweater or shoes and perhaps learn to care for a pet through imagery, with verbal guidance by a parent or teacher.

Cooling Off

Learning to Remove My Coat is a life-skills and science-related exercise teaching body-awareness. It addresses the Bodily-Kinesthetic, Linguistic, Visual-Spatial and Intrapersonal Intelligences.

The weather is getting cold again. What season is it?...We will do an exercise today to learn how to remove our coats. What sometimes happens when we try to remove our coats?...The arms get stuck? or turn wrong-side out?...Let's practice together by removing our coats in an imagery exercise. Stand up in the circle. Get plenty of room between you and the next person...and let your eyes close.

Imagine that we have just come into this cozy, warm room from playing outside. Our coats are much too warm and heavy, so we begin to remove them. First, let's undo any fasteners. Unbutton the buttons, or unzip the zipper, or untie any other fasteners...In your imagination, and without moving from where you are, do that now...Good. Now, lift your coat from around your shoulders and let it slide down behind your back. Your arms are still in it...Now reach one hand across to the opposite sleeve edge and gently pull it off that arm. Do that slowly now...Have you done that now?...Good. Then what? Yes, just reach across in front of you now to the other sleeve edge and gently pull it off that arm...Great! Now, in your imagination, take your coat in your hand and walk to where you will hang it...Do that now. Carefully hang your coat so that it won't fall to the floor...Very good. With your eyes still closed, look at the row of coats hanging nicely on the hooks...Can you see all the colors?...What color is your coat?...Are there many different sizes and shapes of coats hanging there?...Do you notice anything else?...Now, let's open our eyes, walk over and get our coats and bring them back to the circle where we'll practice what we've just imagined.

What Comes First?

This exercise is written for a slightly more advanced group than that for which the previous exercise was written. It involves the "Removal-of-Coats" exercise, which is also effective with an older group because it provides a focus upon concentration and awareness. The following imagery addresses order: what comes first, second, and so on. Designed as a math exercise, it involves the Logical-Mathematical, Linguistic, Visual-Spatial, Bodily-Kinesthetic and Intrapersonal Intelligences.

Recall the exercise where we used imagery to remove our coats...We concentrated on each movement necessary to remove our coats...Now I ask you to recall those movements. So...relaxing again, as we always do...give your body complete permission to relax...Recognize that your mind is very alert...Take a few moments to do that now...

Good. Now, let's begin to recall the steps, the movements, for us to remove our coats. What did we do first?...[We stood in a circle.] What was second?...[We closed our eyes.] We used eight steps to remove our coats. Do your best to recall as many of those movements, or steps, as you can...and put them in order. First...second...third...forth...and so on...And do that now...

Good. Now, take the pencil and paper that we have brought here for this purpose, and write down the steps that it takes to remove our coats. Do that now...

Okay. Did anyone recall half the steps? Four of the steps? Good. Did anyone recall more? Great. Will someone read to us your list of the steps it took for us to remove our coats?

A Memory Device   ✚ ⬦ ⚘ ⬦

This exercise ties in with the previous two. It can be used with middle-elementary through adult ages. I have lost its source, but I learned it in a workshop or a class. Dealing with order, memorization, mental exploration and manipulation of objects, it can be used as a math exercise. Helpful in areas where memorization of a list is necessary, it involves the Linguistic, Logical-Mathematical, Visual-Spatial, and Bodily-Kinesthetic Intelligences.

You will need pencil, paper and a partner. Get them now, and sit with your partner. Your first task is to number 1-10 and to list ten random objects in those spaces. Do not let your partner see your list. Turn your paper face-down and hand it to your partner, without looking at the words .

Now, with your partner's paper still face-down, number 1 to 10 on the back and write down ten places in your home. Begin with the front door and move *in order* **through your house. Do your best not to backtrack. Just keep moving, in order, through your house. List ten places in your house.** [Example: living room wall, sofa, hallway...]

In a minute, when I ask you to do so, but not yet, you will turn the paper over. Not using your pencil, but using your imagination... make mental images of these places in your house...you will put each object listed by your partner into the places in your house. That is, the object listed by your partner as #1 will be imaged in place #1 in your house. The object listed as #2 will be imaged in place #2...and so on throughout the list. As you visualize them see them as clearly as you can. This will be a timed game, so when I tell you to stop, please do so, but do not speak. Questions? Okay...Begin. [Announce a set amount of time. Usually one minute is sufficient.]

Stop now. Without speaking, and when I tell you to do so, you will look at the side of the paper that *you* **wrote, the one where you listed places in your home. Again, as I time you for one minute, write the objects that you imaged beside the names of the places. That is, if your #1 is the front door, and your #1 object was a candy-bar, write candy-bar beside front door. Questions?... Begin now.**

Stop! Okay. Check and see how many you got correct. Did anyone get 7? 8? More? All of them? Great! What you have found out is that you can memorize ten things in one minute if you have "hooks" or places upon which to hang your images. You could memorize many more, using the same framework. Just go back and hang images of new objects on the old ones...on and on. Yes, it does help,

doesn't it? Try it the next time you must memorize a list of things. Just remember to *order* the places in your house (no backtracking) and clearly visualize the objects you are memorizing. Then write them down. Time yourself. Good luck!

Pet Care

A lesson in the interdependence of living things, this is designed as a science lesson that addresses the Interpersonal, Bodily-Kinesthetic, Logical-Mathematical and Visual-Spatial Intelligences.

We have been studying how all living things depend upon each other, are interdependent. We know how the plants depend upon all the organic matter in the earth, how the corn plant grows tall and depends upon the bees to help it to pollinate so that the corn forms, and so on. Today we will look at how our pets depend upon us. How many of you help to take care of your pets? (Brief pets discussion follows.)

Let's do an imagery exercise today to imagine all the ways that our dog or cat or bird or hamster depends upon us. So let your eyes close...and for a few minutes just feel yourself sitting there...Feel the rug under you...Feel your crossed legs...Feel your arms and hands...just notice them now...Feel your head and your eyes...Feel your neck and your back...and even your tummy, too. Notice how very strong you feel. Good. Now, for a few minutes, let's pretend that we aren't who we really are, but we are our own pets. Think of how it feels to *be* your pet dog...or cat...or whatever kind of pet you have...In your imagination, move around the room as your pet...and notice how it is to walk on four legs instead of two...Notice how it is to be hairy or furry on this warm day...Do you feel warm now?...Would you like some water to drink?...Run over to your bowl ...Is there water there? No? Who will get water for you?...Is there food in your food bowl? Who will feed you, now that you are getting hungry?...Oh, here comes your friend to feed you. You really depend upon your friend to do that, don't you? You can't get food and water by yourself, can you? Now, for the next little bit of time, think of the ways that you, as a pet, depend upon your friend to help you and to care for you...

Now, think what you, as a pet, do for your friend who cares for you...

Good. Now, slowly become a person again...the very person you always are...and open your eyes...Be back in this room, sitting on the floor with your legs crossed, and let's talk about how we and our pets depend upon one another...

After a learning experience on growing edible plants, you might design an exercise that would carry the child's awareness throughout the complete farming cycle. Starting with the plant and watching the harvest, then moving to food preparation and ending with the effect of nutrition on healthy, strong bodies that again sow seeds for nutritious edible plants. This teaches the child about interdependence and also stresses the whole cycle, instead of only the parts of the cycle. This whole process encourages a more complete understanding than in more traditionally taught lessons in which the parts may never be understood in relationship to one another.

"Growing Like a Weed" or a Plant!

This is a lesson in how things change as they grow, how they are interdependent, and an experience of the whole cycle of growing things. It is designed as a science lesson that addresses the Bodily-Kinesthetic, Verbal-Linguistic, Visual-Spatial, and Intrapersonal Intelligences.

Today is the day when we can go outside and transplant our small plants that are growing well in the little cups where we planted them. What do you think will happen to them when we plant them outside? They will grow? Yes. They will get wet when it rains? Yes, that, too. (And so on...) **Tell me what has happened since you**

planted those seeds in the little cups? You watered them? Yes. You watched them? Yes, you did! They just grew up through the soil? Yes, they did that, too. They grew leaves? Absolutely!

Well, let's spend a few minutes in imagery before we go outside, imagining ourselves to be those plants...and let's see what happens. Okay? Let's stretch out on the rug today...on your tummies. Just rest there...feeling very relaxed...very much like the little seed might have felt, if it could feel, as it lay in the soft soil in your cup. Just rest there...waiting. Someone has put the cup into the window and the warm sunshine is warming you, little seed. As the soil begins to get dry from the sun, someone waters you...Ah...doesn't that cool water feel wonderful!...

You begin to feel the warmth and the moist soil more and more...And you feel your seed-skin beginning to split a bit...Oh no, it doesn't hurt...In fact, you may feel happy because you know something new is happening to you...And as your seed-skin splits a bit more you realize that a small sprout is beginning to grow from the center of you...You are that sprout...and you begin to grow...very slowly...Just imagine yourself begininning to grow now...

Someone waters you again, and the warm sun seems to be calling to you to stretch upward...and you do begin to grow and to reach upward toward the sun...and POP!...You seem to throw off your soil cover. You pop right out of it, and begin to reach slowly upward...right up toward the sunshine. For the next minute or so, just feel yourself slowly growing upward...and upward...feeling the wonderful sunshine on you...Feel the water...and the soil at your feet...You grow on and on...while I just wait for a minute...

Now you are big enough to be taken outside in the garden and planted there to grow. How do you feel about that?...In your imagination, how do you feel about going to live in the garden? Someone is very carefully carrying the cup that is your home...You are going outside to live in the garden! Very, very carefully, they lift you, and the soil, out of the cup...and place you into the garden spot they have already dug and prepared for you...Very carefully...they pull the new soil up around the old...and you begin to feel very different. How do you feel now?...Is there a lot of room? Do you have plenty of room in which you can grow?...What else do you notice now?...In your imagination, notice all that you can about being a plant in a new garden...It is raining...And now the sun comes out again...The children have come out to play and to look at you...What is that like?

Remember all that you can about being a tiny seed...a small plant in a cup...and then a plant that lives and grows in the new garden...Very slowly now...stop being a plant and become the person that you really are...Find yourself back in this room, getting ready to take your own plants outside.

When we come back into this room, we can paint stories about our plants. Okay? Let's go, then...taking the plants outside, carefully.

Dinosaurs

An exercise in recalling what we know about dinosaurs, this is designed as a science lesson and addresses the Verbal-Linguistic, Musical, Visual-Spatial, Bodily-Kinesthetic and Personal Intelligences.

Today we will go on an imaginary science expedition. So, gather all the things you will need to take with you so that you can bring back information from your trip into the distant past. Today we will go on a dinosaur hunt! What will you need to take with you? Pencil? Paper? Pith helmet? Binoculars? Cameras? Something to measure things? A compass? What else? Remember you must carry all the things that you take, and also bring them all back with you.

Okay, are we ready now? Then just sit or lie down and let your mind begin to relax...to get ready for an adventure...relaxing now...And let your body relax, too, so that it will be strong and ready to take you on this journey...just letting your whole body relax now...Feel yourself relaxed...supported by the floor...completely relaxed...and alert...

It is the day for our dinosaur hunt. Gather those things that you have selected to bring with you...bringing your "time-watch," as well, so that we may see on its special face how far into the distant past we are reaching...And, as we look at the time-watch, we see its hands begin to move into the past...to 1900...1500...1000...500 ...10...1000 BC...5000 BC...back...and back...to the Cenozoic period...and on back...all the way into the Mesozoic period...when the great dinosaurs roamed the land. Find yourself there now...with your classmates...and your teacher...We are all there now...visiting this ancient time before people lived on this land...We are here in the land of the dinosaur.

As our scientific assignment on this expedition, you recall that we are to find all the types of dinosaurs, record their sizes, sounds, foods and everything about their habitats. We will also record anything

else you notice or discover about these great reptiles. You have three minutes of actual clock time to do that. It is equal to all the time you will need. Begin to do that now. [Wait for three minutes]

Now it is time to leave the land and time of the great dinosaurs, having had a great adventure, and having gathered much important information to take back into our own time...to share with others. Let's thank those enormous reptiles for allowing us to visit them safely...and begin our long time-trek home again.

Looking at our time-watches, see the hands beginning to move back toward our own time, but slowly at first...See them move from the Mesozoic period...to the Cenozoic...then faster...and faster...to 1000 BC...to 500 BC...10 AD...500 AD...See them slowing down again...to 1000...1500...1900...and back to your time...to our classroom...Finding yourself here now, open your eyes and without talking yet, take out your paper and write a story about your adventure and what you found.

You may wish to read some of the stories aloud or to have an open discussion after the writing is completed. An art lesson in clay sculpture would be a very appropriate follow-up for this exercise.

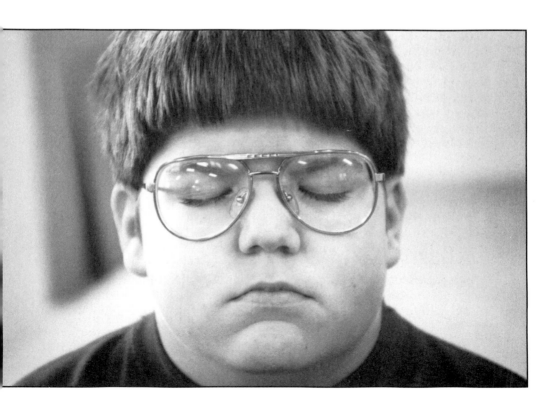

"Truth or Consequences" or
Kings Can Be Foolish, Too!

A lesson in the consesquences of actions, this exercise is written as an integrated Social Studies and English lesson. It addresses the Verbal-Linguistic and Personal Intelligences.

Using a story or fable, such as <u>The Emperor's New Clothes</u> by Hans Christian Anderson, read a large part of the story. Let the children complete the story first in imagery and then in writing. Having prepared the children for an imagery exercise, read the entire story to this point:

(Story)   **"None of the emperor's clothes had been**
so successful before.

'But he has got nothing on,' said a little child.

'Oh, listen to the innocent,' said its father; and
one person whispered to the other what the
child had said. 'He has nothing on; a child
says he has nothing on!'

'But he has nothing on!' at last cried all of the people.

The emperor..."

Continue the story in your imaginations now. Describe what might have happened to the emperor because of his foolish actions...his foolish pride. What might have happened to the others who also "saw" the beautiful clothes as they were made and as the procession began? What might have happened to the child who spoke the truth? What could have happened to the others? Take a few minutes now to complete this funny story in your imagination. When you finish...being really certain that your story *is* finished...take your pencil and write the ending you have imagined for this story. Do that now...

Another example of an imagery exercise in which literature is used for imaginative discovery follows:

The Bears and Me: Feelings

A lesson to increase empathy by imagining the feelings of others, this imagery exercise is designed as a social studies lesson and addresses the Verbal-Linguistic, Visual-Spatial, Bodily-Kinesthetic and Personal Intelligences.

Having prepared the children for an imagery exercise, begin reading
The Story of the Three Bears (author uncertain). Read to the point where
it says:

> **"By this time the Three Bears thought their**
> **porridge would be cool enough for them to eat**
> **it properly, so they came home for breakfast.**
> **Now careless Goldilocks had left the spoon of**
> **the Great Big Bear standing in his porridge.**
> **'SOMEBODY HAS BEEN AT MY PORRIDGE!'**
> **said the Great Big Bear in his great, rough gruff voice."**

**In your imaginations, how do you think the Great Big Bear felt
about someone having eaten part of his breakfast?...How would you
feel if you came down to breakfast and someone had eaten part of
your breakfast?...**

Continue asking about the Middle-Sized Bear...the Little Wee
Bear...and on through the story. As an exercise on consequences of
actions, ask **"What do you think happened to Goldilocks for doing
what she did? What would happen to you if you did such a thing?"**
These questions not only help the children to put themselves into the
place of another, but also shed insight into their perceptions of
punishment at home. With the increasing prevalence of child-abuse, this
can help teachers to recognize whether abuse may be occurring. It can
help parents to know how their children feel and how they perceive
punishment.

Another exercise that helps children to build a sense of self and helps
to support their new confidence is one that uses art in making
comparisons, contrasting, choosing and self-discovery.

Me, Myself and Others

A lesson in noticing likenesses and differences in families and friends,
this is designed as a social studies and art lesson. It addresses the
Personal, Visual-Spatial, Bodily-Kinesthetic and Verbal-Linguistic
Intelligences.

Having prepared the children for an imagery exercise, have them lie
on the floor (if possible) and relax...

**Today, let's imagine ourselves. Can you see YOU in your
imagination?...What do you look like?...How tall are you?...Are
you smiling or frowning?...What color is your hair? Your eyes?**

...Can you see your ears?...How about your nose?...How many teeth do you have? Are some missing now?...Do you have some small ones and some larger ones?...Feel how your chin and your neck grow together...Feel your arms...are they long? Strong?...Right at the end of your arms...what? Hands! How many fingers do you have? Count them now...Good. Do you have on any jewelry or decorations?...Did I hear a tummy growl? Are you hungry now?...Notice how your tummy feels...your back, too, as you rest on the floor...Notice your buttocks and your hips...can your hips move easily to help you run?...Are your legs long?...Notice your feet...feel how flexible they are..."Flexible" is a big word. What does it mean?...Are your feet "flexible?"...How many toes have you?...Are they tight in your shoes or do they have lots of room to move?...What are you wearing?...What would you *like* to be wearing?...If we were to paint a portrait of this YOU that we've been describing, in what place would you be in the painting?...Who would be with you?...Can you see them there, too? Are they tall like you?...Do they have the same color hair and eyes as you do? Do they look like you?...How do they look?...What are they wearing?...Do they like being in this picture with you?...Are they smiling?...Would you have anyone else with you?...a pet?...a favorite toy?...Would you choose anything else to be in your portrait?...Is it just as you like it? Good. When you are ready, open your eyes and go to the tables and paint the portrait you have imagined...with all the things you have imagined in it. Be sure to include you! Do that now...

Backward and Forward

An exercise to build awareness and control of body movement, this is designed as a lesson in physical education. It addresses the Bodily-Kinesthetic, Verbal-Linguistic, Visual-Spatial and Intrapersonal Intelligences. Thanks to Dr. Gay Luce, who introduced me to this kind of exercise.

This exercise is different from other imagery exercises in that you will be moving your body at the same time that you are imaging your body in movement. The actual and imagined movements will *not* be identical. Standing straight and with an arms-length between you and the people on either side and in front of you, and letting your eyes close gently, begin to be aware of your body...Begin to let each part of your body release any stress or tension that may be there today...Start with your feet, your calves, knees, thighs, buttocks, and your hips... [Stop momentarily between each body part to give the imagizers time to bring each part clearly into their awareness.] Notice your lower back...your belly, and your chest, upper back, shoulders, neck, back of your head, your face, eyes, mouth, tongue...your upper arms, lower arms, wrists, hands, and fingers...Feel each part of your body completely free from tension...relaxed. You have no stress at all...

Take three steps forward now...slowly...just take three slow steps forward. As you take these three steps forward, think carefully about what your body is doing. Feel the movements you are making...in every small detail. Feel the three steps forward as you take them...Good. Now do the same thing, except that your three steps are three steps backward...Take just three steps backward...slowly...noticing each movement in detail...Take three steps backward...noticing....

Now, repeat those steps...three steps forward...three steps backward...being certain to notice each movement that your body makes to propel you...three steps forward, then three steps backward. Do that three complete times...that is, three steps forward and three steps backward *three times each*.... Do that now. [Wait until the participants have completed this set of movements.]

Standing still now...and recalling what you have just done...notice, recalling each detail. Begin again to take three steps forward. *But*...as you take the three steps forward, you will *imagine* yourself to be taking three steps backward! Your "actual" body will take three steps forward while your "imaginary" body will take three steps backward. Do that now...as slowly as is necessary...Take three steps forward with your "actual" body and three steps backward with your "imaginary" body...at the same time.

Reversing that now, take three steps backward with your "actual" body while your "imaginary" body takes three steps forward. Slowly, now...move as slowly as you must, to do this with complete awareness...Good.

Now, slowly, and observing your movements very carefully, repeat that whole process two more times. That is, take three steps forward with your "actual" body and three steps backward with your "imaginary" body. Then, reverse that. Take three steps backward with your "actual" body and three steps forward with your "imaginary" body. Do that whole process a total of three times. Do that now...Slowly...Good.

Now just gently sit where you are...and, as you are ready, open your eyes. How was that for you? Why was it so different? Was it difficult? Why do you think that was so? Did it become easier as you progressed? Could you image each movement? Were there many more movements than you thought there would be? So, you are learning to "do two things at once." Many people say that they often do that, or that they must do it. You are learning to *control* doing more than one thing at a time. You are learning to think of two things at once while you control your movements. Can you imagine how that might be helpful to you in sports...or dance? It has been shown that the ability to image movement in sports increases one's performance greatly. If you are not in sports, or dance, how might this exercise help you? Could you teach it to someone else now?

Shape and Form: Transformation

In some exercises, we use one intelligence in the service of another. In this math lesson focusing on geometric forms, we visualize shapes which become forms. This uses the Visual-Spatial Intelligence in service of the Logical-Mathematical Intelligence. It also addresses the Intrapersonal Intelligence.

We have been learning about solid geometric figures. Today our exercise will examine those figures and also others. First, begin as we always do, by relaxing...letting your body relax. Turn loose any stress...or tiredness...or anything at all that is keeping you from being totally aware...totally alert...completely conscious of what we will be thinking...Just relax now...

A long time ago, we learned about shapes, two-dimensional shapes, such as squares...circles...triangles...and rectangles...Recall each of those as you image them now...

Recently, we have studied three-dimensional forms, geometric figures. In your mind's eye, imagine a two dimensional square becoming a three dimensional form. What would it become...a cube?...Right. And a circle? What would it become as it becomes three-dimensional? A sphere? Right...A triangle? Cone? Right...

Select one of the geometric forms we have just identified. Place it, as you image it, in front of you. Now raise it up just a little bit, about a foot higher...but still in front of you. Pretending that it is very light in weight, blow hard on it and watch as it moves up into the air above your head...two, three or four feet higher. Watch it move.

What happens to it as it moves upward? Now watch as it begins to descend...Watch it as it falls down, lightly, and lands gently upon your nose.

Take it now in your imaginary hands...and watch as it changes into a different object made from that form. If you are holding a cube, it may become...what? If you are holding a sphere?...A cone?...Allow that to happen slowly now. Watch as the geometric form transforms into some object that is made from it...Good. Now, looking closely at that object, take your imaginary pencil and draw a picture of that object...and then color it. You have enough time to do it, and so do that now while I am silent...Good...

Now, still holding the object and looking at your drawing, let the object revert to the simple geometric form. Look at the geometric figure, and draw it beside your other drawing...And then, watch as the geometric form again reduces itself to a two-dimensional shape...right there, in your hand. Draw it, too...beside the other two drawings...

When you finish, just let your eyes open, and take your real pencil and paper and draw (and color) those same drawings that you created in your imagination. Do that now...

New Caps for Old ✛ ⬥ ⚓ ⚖

This exercise is named for a children's book. It is adapted from several exercises taught by Tony Buzan in a workshop and by Roger van Oechs in his writings. An exercise in creative thinking, it asks that you take an ordinary object and think of as many uses for it as you can imagine. I have used it often with students to get them to think outside the "givens." It utilizes intuition and logic in a creative synthesis and involves a wide range of intelligences, including Logical-Mathematical, Verbal-Linguistic, and the Personal Intelligences. Most important, it is pleasurable. I believe pleasure is a major motivating factor in learning.

Reach into your pocket, or purse, and grab a handful of things you find there and put them out on your table (or desktop). Now let's look through these things and select one, something ordinary, that we use often.

Okay, here is something. May we use this one? Here is an old stub of a pencil. How long do you estimate it to be? Three inches? Four inches? Okay. Just look at this very plain object, an old pencil stub. Everybody here probably has one. Right? Well, for a full minute of clock time, equal to "all the time we need," let's imagine things we can do with this pencil. Just close your eyes, and as I keep track of time, think of as many things as possible that we could do with this pencil. Begin now...

Okay. I'll bet you had a long list, yes? Will somebody write a list of our suggestions on the board? Thank you. Okay, who has an idea of something we can do with this pencil? One at a time, now, so we can write the list on the board...

Write with it...write a story...keep score at the game...take a test...jab it through paper...chew on it...put a propeller on it and spin it...paint it another color...sharpen it...get it a new eraser...show it to my friends...take it home with me...throw it away...get some more and build something with them...scrape off the paint...hold your hair up with it...make earrings out of it, if you cut it in half...get another one and make long earrings...roll it...race another pencil...and so on and on.

Most groups, with a little encouragement can go on indefinitely. While the enthusiasm for invention is maintained, let them continue. It is a good lesson in not letting what we already know limit what we can imagine, invent or dream.

Moving in Space

An exercise designed for dance or music education, this one allows the imager to experience movement in the kinesthetic body or the body of muscular imagination. It addresses the Visual-Spatial, Bodily-Kinesthetic and Musical Intelligences.

Lying on the floor, let the floor support you and let your body begin to relax...Let all the tiredness drain out. Let it drain out right through the floor and into the earth, where it can become restored. Relax each part of your body...noticing as you scan your body if every part *is* relaxed...How about your neck? Your toes? The small of your back? And so on...

As you are feeling yourself relaxed...and refreshed...I will play a tape of some music. [Use a Windham Hill recording by George Winston or whatever you like.] **As you listen to the music, feel yourself becoming a part of the music...perhaps all of the music...You feel its rhythms...its sounds...its silences...**

As you become a part of the music (or all of the music), let yourself feel the music's shape. Is it curved? or angular? What is its shape? In your mind, move your body to form the shape of the music. Just move, as a part of the music...and become whatever shape you feel this music to be...

Notice the quality of the space within which you are moving with this music...Is it your personal space? Is it a somewhat general space? What is the space like?...How do your body shapes fit into this music-space?...

Does the music move upward? Downward? Forward? Backward? In what direction does the shape of this music move?...What happens to the music-space as the shapes move? Does it change?...

Continue moving your body as the music plays....In your imagination, form the shapes of the music...form the shapes within the music-space.   Continue now until I stop the music...

Stop now. Do not open your eyes, or get up yet, and I will change the music we are hearing. This music will be different from the last. [Perhaps a march tune or a clashing synthesizer sound-piece.] **As you listen to it...while it is playing...repeat the process you have just done but this time respond to the new music...**

Becoming a part of this music...or all of the music...feel yourself becoming one with the sounds...Good. Again, notice the shapes of the music...Are they curved shapes? or angular ones? What shape is this music?...

In your imagination, allow yourself to move into the shapes of this music. Notice the music-space and observe it to see if it changes as you move within it...Is it personal space? or more general space? What is the music-space like?...As it moves upward or downward, forward or backward, what happens to the music-space? Does it change?...What happens to it as you move within it?...

Again, as the music continues, let your kinesthetic body move with the music, forming the shapes of the music...within the music-space. And continue that until I stop you...

Stop now...Bringing yourself slowly back into a relaxed state... recall all that you have just observed and experienced about these two forms of music. Staying silent, just get up slowly...

As I start the music again, let your real body move about the room, forming the shapes of this first music...and later as I play the second music...Recall it and experience it again, expressing all that you have discovered about these two different musical forms.

You've Got Rhythm

This exercise is designed for both music and movement education and emphasizes beat or rhythm. It increases awareness of the qualities of sounds and addresses the Musical, Bodily-Kinesthetic and Visual-Spatial Intelligences.

As you lie down, I will play recordings of environmental sounds... sounds from nature...and from cities. As each sound plays, notice its own particular and unique rhythms...

As you listen, and as you feel the rhythm of each recording I play for you, find a drum in your imagination...Find one that you like...one that you know you can play without any difficulty at all. You can play it softly...or with great energy and strength...You can play it in whatever way you need to play it to express the rhythm of the music you are hearing at the time.

So, as you begin to relax...every part of your body...Relax your mind, and at the same time, feel your alertness...Pay attention to the music that you hear...[Play environmental music now, perhaps the wind or heartbeat music, in some way provide a soft, gentle, relaxed sound.]

Listening now...hear the beat...the pulse...the rhythm of this sound...Pick up your imaginary drum...and using your hand or a drum stick, or whatever you know will be the most appropriate instrument for making the rhythms of this sound, begin to play your drum now...[Change to the next sound, perhaps the sound of crashing ocean waves or a hawk's or crow's scream. Use a more intense sound than the first, but not an extreme example, yet.]

Listen now...hear the beat of this sound...its pulse...its rhythm...Use your drum again...and strike the appropriate rhythm for this sound. Do that now...[Then, use a third sound, perhaps the sound of a thunderstorm or the sounds of traffic in a city. The sounds should be loud and sharp now.]

Again, listen...Notice how differently you may feel as you listen to these sounds...Discover the beat, the pulse, the rhythm of *these* sounds...Again, strike your imaginary drum in a way that is appropriate to these sounds. Just imagine yourself doing that now...Good.

Now, leaving your drum and the sounds, as I turn the volume lower and lower, return to your space on this floor, in this room. As you are ready, allow your eyes to open. Sit up...and stretch a bit.

How was that for you? Could you feel the rhythms? Were they similar? Were they different from each other? Can you compare them in words? Are they easier to compare with drums? With pictures?

Imagine the Sound of a Snowflake

This exercise is designed for music education. It combines visual and auditory images. My thanks to Don Campbell for some of the images in this exercise, which were inspired by his book, Introduction to the Musical Brain. It addresses the Musical and Intrapersonal Intelligences.

Today I will read some words to you. As I do, notice the pictures that you make in your mind's eye. For instance, imagine the sound of a snowflake falling...Sit comfortably and allow your body to relax...even though your brain remains very active. As I mention things that you can recognize by sight, imagine what sound or sounds they make. When I mention things you can recognize by sound, imagine what those sounds would look like. Now you can completely relax...

Imagine the sound of a whale...Imagine the sound of a whisper...what would a whisper look like...What sound would a river make, and what picture would you see if you heard that sound? A cave?...A drop of rain?...Imagine the sound of a ray of light...of laughter...of chewing gum...What is the sound of dreaming?...of wet grass after a storm?...of a newborn baby?... Imagine the sound of someone snoring and what that would look like...or shouting...What is the sound of eating popcorn?...of a jet plane?...of a harmonica?...What might those sounds look like?...What is the sound of your friend's voice?...of a computer?...Can you picture those sounds too?...Imagine a scary sound...And a happy sound...What sound would mean "hurry?"...What sound could greet a neighbor?...What does "goodbye" sound like?...Think of the nicest sound you can imagine...and keep thinking of it until I ask you to stop...Do that now...Stop now...and let's discuss the sounds you heard. Did any sound have color? Shape? Rhythm? Can you remember what your favorite sound was? Picture it again in your mind and then you may draw that picture of your favorite sound. Color it, too. Later, we will share our drawings with each other.

Musical Memories ♪ ♫ ♬

A similar exercise appears in Don Campbell's <u>Introduction to The Musical Brain,</u> as well as in Jean Houston's <u>The Possible Human.</u> Thanks to both of them for the inspiration for this exercise. It addresses the Musical and Personal Intelligences.

Sit down beside a partner. Allow your eyes to close. One of you will ask the questions that I suggest and the other will answer. Then, after several questions, I will ask you to exchange roles. So, please decide who will be "Asker" first. The other will be the first "Answerer".

As you relax your body...let your eyes relax and gently close... Recall, now, some of your memories of sounds and of music... "Asker," please ask your partner, "Do you remember clapping rhythms? Tell me about them." And, "Answerer," answer aloud now...Ask, "Do you remember singing in the car as you went on a trip?"..."A song someone sang to you as a child?"..."Your elementary school band?"..."The voice of someone you love?"...

Please change roles now. Ask, "Do you remember the sound of a metronome?"..."Do you remember teaching a song to a friend?"..."Sitting in someone's lap who sang to you?"..."Your music teacher's voice?"... "The voice of someone you love?"...

Take a few minutes now, until I ask you to stop, to talk with your partner about your musical memories. Do that now...(Allow about 3-4 minutes, depending upon the ages of the participants. Then take time to see if anyone would like to share their experiences in musical memory with the group.)

Music Makers ♪ ☞ ♫ ♬

This exercise is designed for an improvisational music lesson. It teaches tolerance and cooperation with others through music making and it increases self-esteem. My debt of gratitude goes to Paul Winter for giving me a healthy dose of self-confidence in his improvisational music workshop. This exercise addresses the Musical, Verbal-Linguistic and Personal Intelligences.

Your assignment was to locate and bring with you some kind of instrument with which to make musical sounds. You need not already know how to play it. The instrument needn't even be traditional. You may have chosen something you simply found and with which you can make sounds, such as rocks or sticks. Some of

you may have brought instruments from home. Some of you may have selected instruments from our "grab box" of various instruments. [I keep drum sticks, small wooden flutes and recorders, harmonicas, rattles, whistles, an ocarina, a kalimba, a tambourine etc. in a large box for playful experimentation.] Others may have been inventive and made their instruments.

Okay, get into groups of four. Be sure your best friends are *not* in your group. That is, form a group with the people you know less well than others. Bring one of your instruments with you. Just sit on the floor with your group, forming a tight little circle...leaving just enough room in the center for knees and instruments...Good.

Take a few minutes to introduce your instrument to your friends, without using any words at all. Just make sounds with your instrument. Try it, one at a time...I think you can hear each other better that way!

Now...use your instrument to say hello to your group. Start with the person facing me...and move clockwise around your circle...Do that now. Just say "Hello"...Now say "Good Morning Friends" with your instrument...without talking...just with your instrument...Going around the circle..."speak" one at a time. Now, all together, say "Good Morning Everybody"...All together now, do it again: "Good Morning Everybody." Okay!

Now, without moving out of the circle...but just sitting as you are...let your eyes close for a few minutes...Relax as you do so...Even if you have never played an instrument before, feel yourself able to play wonderful musical sounds...Hear the sounds that the instruments in your circle make, and know that the range of each one is broader than you have heard yet. Each may be louder, or softer, (or other variations) so let yourself imagine "words" that you might say to your group...with your instrument...What answers might your group give to you?...Your group will answer as a whole...not individually, but as a group. Imagine that now...as your eyes open again, staying silent...

Beginning with whomever was second in order during the last exercise, play the message you imagined. Whether or not your group understands it as you understand it, they will answer you. Listen to their answers very carefully. Do that now...

Okay now! You are "talking with your instruments," communicating with your music. Take a minute and describe what your message was, and listen as your group tells you what they answered...in words this time.

Taking turns now, each one, individually...tell your group something with your instrument and listen to their answers. Then, briefly, discuss each one...but not until after you have completed the musical communication. Do that now, taking about five minutes for each set...

Stop now. You sounded great! Which group will share what you found out with this whole room full of musicians? [Take the time to let each group share its experiences.]

Now, exchanging instruments, taking an instrument that is not the one you have been using, move into groups of six and I will give you further instructions.

Instructions can range from a complete sense of play, such as telling a short joke with the instruments, to something serious, like making the sounds of prayer or the sounds of personal feelings. After the group has left their self-consciousness behind, they may choose their own "mood" or attitude within this framework.

"If You Don't Know Where You're Going, You'll End Up Somewhere Else"

This exercise, named for a book I read many years ago, uses imagery to encourage the examination of goals. It can be used in many different ways, with different age groups and in many different disciplines. I have used it recently in working with a group of adult cardiac patients in a rehabilitation program at a nearby university. The patients are from a variety of backgrounds and have different needs. This exercise is broadly designed to meet the variety of needs in a group. You may wish to narrow it for your own use. It addresses several intelligences, but particularly the Personal Intelligences.

Some of you have told me that you find it difficult to relax. So, let's begin this exercise not by *trying* to relax, but just *letting* our bodies relax. Begin by getting comfortable...and breathing. Easy enough? Just be comfortable...and breathe naturally...noticing your comfort...and noticing your breath...it goes in...and it comes out...in...and out...just breathe for a little longer...in...and out...

Next, relax your feet. Wiggle your feet around a little bit...and turn them loose...just turn them completely loose. And your ankles...roll them around...and then relax them...your calves...tense them...and relax them. Your knees...move them just a bit...and then let them go...relaxing them completely. Notice how your legs feel...is there any tension remaining there? Let it go...Give your legs complete permission to relax. Your thighs and buttocks...tighten your muscles a little bit...then relax them. Your lower back, do the same...tense it a little bit...then relax it. Many people hold a lot of tension in their upper back and shoulders. Move yours around now...and then let them go. Know that the mat and the floor will support you... completely relax. Your stomach...for now...just relax it. Relax your chest...take a deep breath and let it out slowly...letting your chest relax. Notice your neck. Roll your head around on your neck and notice any tension or soreness there. Now let it go...let all of the soreness and all of the tension go. Let your neck relax. Your head...the back of your head and over the top of your scalp...just let it relax. Feel your forehead...let it droop...relax...all of the alert-forehead look is gone for a little while as you relax your eyes. Open your mouth wide, letting it remain open a little as it relaxes. Even your tongue...just let it relax. Let your arms relax...and your hands...and each finger, too. Be completely relaxed...feeling wonderful and completely relaxed.

Now, while you are feeling so relaxed, and your mind is alert, think about the goals you have set for yourself. Each of you has set goals for yourself, personal goals, that you hope to reach...in a short time...in several months...in a couple of years. These goals will aid in your health...They will result in your having excellent health. Think about your goals for a minute...Select one of your goals now...whether it is to become a non-smoker, to lose weight or to work on changing your responses to job stress or family stress...Perhaps your goal is to go hiking or fishing...or to play with your grandchildren...Whatever your goal is for yourself, spend the next minute of clock time experiencing the goal *as if it has happened for you.* That is, feel yourself doing it, as you pick up your last cigarette...knowing it *is* your last one because smoking really does not appeal to you...It is very distasteful...in fact, you are putting that last cigarette out...throwing it away...and feeling very good for having done so. Knowing, now, how great you feel to be free from tobacco addiction...feeling great...breathing more deeply than you have in a long time...Notice, for the first time in many months or even years, how wonderful things smell...and taste. You are free from cigarettes! Know that it is so.

If you are dieting, picture yourself as you would like to look. Be realistic, but definitely see yourself as trimmer, slimmer and more able to get about with ease...Hold that picture in your mind... experience the reality of that picture...fully believe it...free yourself from all doubt...and know that it is the real you.

If you are experiencing stress in your work, at home or elsewhere in your life, picture your situation as you would like it to be. See and hear other people responding as you wish they would...Hear yourself responding clearly...calmly...and with a lot of internal confidence and power...Feel yourself relaxing as you picture your situation improving...Imagine that it is even *good* again...Imagine it exactly as you wish it to be...Practice being like that for a few minutes...

So, whatever your goal, if it is one of the ones mentioned...or something else...build an image of how you want it to be, climb inside the image and experience it as if it were actually happening...Enjoy it. Notice how good it feels. Notice *all* of the details of this event...What do you see? What do you smell? Do you hear anything? How does your body feel? What kind of thoughts are you having? Do your best to notice and remember everything...(one minute).

These are exercises that you can practice on your own. My own experience and the experiences of many other people I know and have worked with attest to the fact that these exercises work. With your participation and committment to their success, your "part in the deal," they will work for you. It is truly so.

Begin to move about a little on the mat...stretching...feeling good, and completely relaxed...Feel yourself ready to move into this new day with a resolve to do your "part in the deal," to watch your goals happen.

Now, letting your eyes open...sit up when you are ready and let's discuss your experiences during this exercise...

The final exercise is one during which you can define or refine your educational vision. I believe that the primary job of education is to encourage and empower each other as well as the children we teach and nurture. The main purpose of this imagery exercise is to encourage you and to allow you to empower *yourself.* I also created this exercise to help you access all the resources within you that you may need to speak your vision aloud in the world.

I will guide you from your own early schooling, with its strengths and its hurts, into your vision of what education could become. I hope that you will find personal ways to express any discoveries you make during this exercise. My vision is that you can use your discoveries and give them form within your educational settings, whether that is at school, at home or in the larger global community.

Education springs from a vision of the future.
Unknown source.

A Personal Vision   ﷼ ⚖

This exercise is adapted from several taught by Dr. Jean Houston during my training at the Foundation for Brain and Mind Research. It focuses upon the recovery of one's own childhood. I have used it and similar ones, with hundreds of different adult groups. It is a powerful exercise because it moves us from the poorest and least enabling parts of our past experiences, into the best and most empowering parts of our future. It addresses the Personal Intelligences.

Use either the relaxation exercise previously noted, or simply recall it in imagery. **Begin by finding a comfortable place to sit...or lie...and just let your eyes close...Breathing slowly, and deeply now...breathe in...and out...in...and out...Continue relaxing each body part in turn, for one minute of clock-time, equal to "all the time you need," and as you breathe fully and freely, begin that now, while I remain silent...**[one minute].

Finding yourself relaxed now...and yet, with your mind very alert...spend a few minutes recalling your childhood impressions of school days. As I guide you in imagery...move into a different time...and a different way of learning. Ask yourself...What is my first school memory? Imagine it now, doing your best to remember all the details...Who are my best friends?...What do we like to do together?...Are there windows here in my childhood school?...Do I enjoy looking out?...Do I like to daydream?...How do the lunches taste?...What is my favorite meal?...Which subjects do I like the best?...The least?...Are there patterns here in my childhood that I recognize in my adult life?...Did I like to move around a lot?...or sit still?...Did I ever have to sit so still that I just couldn't think?...What was my teacher's voice like?...Did she smile a lot?...What color were her eyes? Did *they* smile?...

What was my schooling really like for me? Was there a time, early in my schooling, when I felt dumb? or afraid? or embarassed? or very foolish? How did I feel?...Did it change the way I responded in class?...In other settings?...Can I feel that clearly even now?...Were there other "woundings" in school for me?...If so, feel them now...as clearly as possible...Have I been different, less than my potential self, because of these early feelings?

Moving back in time and space to the present, continue in imagery. As a parent or a teacher of children, I am going to ask you to rewrite that script now that you have recalled your early school "woundings." You, as your current Full Self, can take the responsibility and enjoy the pleasure of nurturing, encouraging and empowering the child that *was* you...In some ways, that child is still *within* you.

Take a minute of clock-time now, equal to "all the time you need," being with your schoolchild self, giving that "child" whatever she or he needs to transform educational problems and "woundings" into new strengths. Remember that you *do* know how...and that you *can*. help your "child" change...Begin to do that now...[one minute].

Now, still within the imagery process, come back to your present day self, and feel the new strengths and encouragement of empowered childhood. Remember once again, that *you know that you can make a difference.* You can make education better for your children...You *can* be the Ideal Parent and the Master Teacher...Imagine...dream now, the ideal school...as you would have it...You are the guide and the teacher...See that now...Experience it all...for the next three minutes of clock-time...while my voice is silent...and until I speak again...[three minutes].

Come back to this space and time...*Now* is the time to offer your vision...to give it form and action in the world. The educational world can no longer afford for you to hold back your visions. The time is now...In a moment, I will ask you to spend some time writing, drawing, dancing, painting or talking your vision. That is the first step toward making your dream a reality. Your primary job is to encourage...to acknowledge...to empower each other and the children that you nurture. My dream is that you believe it...and I know that you now possess all that you need to put your vision into action. *You* are the encouraging and caring parent. You *are* the creative and empowering teacher...It is so...

CONCLUSION

Images bring us into touch with ...general truths which have eternally bound mankind together.   C. Day Lewis

The Lord searcheth all hearts, and understandeth all the imaginations of the thoughts.   Chronicles 28:9.

We stand today on the edge of a new frontier....   John Fitzgerald Kennedy

When I began imagery research, I believed that if teachers and parents became familiar with imagery practice through personal experience and found it to be beneficial, they would begin to use it with their children. Many teachers, parents and children have told me of their imagery experiences and the benefits of those practices in their lives.

Imagery is a natural way of thinking which produces change, often before we are aware of it. Becoming consciously aware of thought through imagery exercises has the potential to help people attain educational and individual life goals. It can be used to address specific curriculum content as well as the environment within which all education occurs. Using imagery to reduce the everyday stresses of modern life can aid people in living healthier, longer lives. Its use can expand our thought processes to encompass much higher levels of thought. The practice of imagery can increase human awareness beyond accustomed levels and guide individuals in the restructure of self-image to achieve their potentials. Because it can assist us in understanding ourselves and others it can be used as a tool to increase happiness and provide a sense of well-being as people use it to achieve their goals.

Dr. Jean Houston puts her vision of the transformation produced by imagistic thought into words as she says, "I see a change. It is vested in the greatest rise in expectations the world has ever seen...I see a change. And you are a part of it."

You *are* a part of it, each of you. Created with the images in your minds, your goals and dreams *can* become reality. The beneficial changes and awarenesses will continue to multiply as you move into the quality future you are helping to create for yourselves and for children, through imagery.

Beholding beauty with the eye of the mind, (we) will be enabled to bring forth...realities.   Plato

ENDNOTES

The imagination I hold to be the living Power and prime Agent of all human Perception and as a repetition in the finite mind of the eternal act of creation... Samuel Taylor Coleridge

I am certain of nothing but...the truth of Imagination – what the imagination seizes as beauty must be truth – whether it existed before or not. John Keats

Acknowledgements

(1) This quotation is from my friend, the Rev. Barbara Brown Taylor, in a personal correspondence as she responded to my request for information relating imagery and theology.

Chapter: Introduction

(1) The history of cognitive psychology is brilliantly reported by Dr. Howard Gardner in <u>The Mind's New Science</u> (1985). The naturalistic, or ecological approach, explained on pages 315-18, is one which centers on

whole processes. Traditionally, only the parts of development, ideas, processes, programs, etc. have been studied, and in isolation from each other in laborotory settings. Bronfenbrenner (1979) points to "the functional interdependence between living organisms and their surroundings." (p. xii) This research approach studies the *normal* behaviors of children in *ordinary* situations with their *usual* caretakers for more natural periods of time. This holistic approach is a natural one for the study of imagery.

Chapter: Research into Imagery

(1) The categories identified as **Beneficial Change for Children Who Practice Imagery** are listed below with specific references for readers who wish for further information:

1. **Increased Enthusiasm** (Singer & Singer, 1985; Houston, 1979; Murdock, 1979).
2. **Better Self-Image** (Fugitt, 1986, 1983; Galyean, 1983b, Lovgren, 1977).
3. **Improved Memory Skills** (Galyean, 1983, 1980; Greeson, 1981; Pressley, 1976; Paivio, 1971).
4. **Greater Respect for Self and Others** (Galyean, 1983c, 1980; Beebe, 1979).
5. **Improved Health** (Galyean, 1982; Rose, 1979).
6. **Greater Mental Flexibility** (Flake, 1986; Filmer & Parkay, 1985; Bagley & Hess, 1984; Roberts, 1981; Rose, 1979).
7. **Expanded Imagination, Creativity and Intuition** (Fillmer & Parkay, 1985; Parrott & Strongman, 1985; Stewart,1985; Bagley & Hess, 1984; Lewis, 1984; Galyean, 1981; Houston, 1979; McKim, 1972).
8. **Improved Thinking Skills** (Frederichs, 1986; Fillmer & Parkay, 1985; Galyean, 1983a, 1982, 1980; Thompson, 1983; O'Regan, 1982; Wachs, 1981; Pressley, 1976;).
9. **Increased Autonomy** (Fugitt, 1986; Galyean, 1983b, 1980; Maslow, 1971).
10. **More Control Over Personal Behavior** (Rose, 1983; Galyean, 1982).
11. **Improved Self-Expression** (Fugitt, 1983; Galyean, 1982; Murdock, 1981;).
12. **Increased Ability to Relax** (Bridges, 1986; Greeson & Zigarmi, 1985; Galyean, 1983c; Frey, 1980;).
13. **Improved Listening Skills** (Galyean, 1983c; Beebe, 1979).
14. **Improved Motor Skills** (Longino, 1987; Achterberg, 1985; Feldenkrais, 1972).
15. **Increased Social Skills** (Galyean, 1983c; Thompson, 1983; Murdock, 1979; Rose, 1979;).
16. **Higher Levels of Personal Satisfaction** (Singer & Singer, 1985; Galyean, 1983b,c).

(2) Morton Hunt is the author of The Universe Within: A New Science Explores the Human Mind. (1982). New York: Simon & Schuster.

(3) Leslie Hart is the author of Human Brain and Human Learning (1983, New York: Longman). He has written several helpful articles that outline his theory of brain-compatible learning. One of the best is "Huge Learning Jumps Show Potency of Brain-based Instruction." Phi Delta Kappan, 68 (2), 143.

(4) Howard Rheingold is a regular contributor to the Institute of Noetic Sciences Newsletter. One of his most inspiring articles is "Imagination and the Importance of Daydreaming," 10 (1), 4-5,20. His article addresses imaginative play, mental imagery and daydreaming in the normal development of children.

(5) Jerome Singer is the author of several books and journals relating to imagery. Partners in Play (1977), Mind-Play (1980) and Make Believe (1985) are among the best. He is also editor for the journal, Imagination, Cognition and Personality: The Scientific Study of Consciousness. In his studies, he identified imagery practice as a benefit of imaginative play during childhood and as an external and internal communication related skill. He calls for the establishment of a science of imagination.

(6) Beverly Galyean's 1983 research repeatedly pointed to the uses of imagery to develop an accelerated mastery of cognitive material. She identified writing skills to be of a significantly higher order. Her research is supported by that of others, including Dr. Robin Beebe (1979), Mary L. Thompson (1983), Robert Rose (1979) and Howard Rheingold (1982).

(7) Frances Vaughn's 1979 book, Awakening Intuition, led the way in reminding readers of the importance of intuition as a way of knowing. It identifies imagery as "the language of intuition."

(8) Constance Kamii was a student of Piaget and remains one who can explain his work with clarity and strength. Her article in Phi Delta Kappan, 65 (6), 410-415, entitled "Autonomy: The Aim of Education Envisioned by Piaget" was superb! Her speech at the SCACUS conference in Columbia, SC in October, 1986 increased my appreciation for her work.

(9) Jacob Bronowski wrote the Yale University Press publication, The Origins of Knowledge and Imagination (1978).

(10) Uri Bronfenbrenner is the author of The Ecology of Human Development.(1979) Cambridge, MA: Harvard University Press. He shows how systems theory applies to education and the developing child: everything relates to everything else. He proposes that today's educators implement "a curriculum for caring."

Chapter: Imagery Exercises

(1) Barbara Clark is the author of Optimizing Learning (1986). Columbus, OH: Merrill. Her book outlines what she calls "The Integrative Education Model in the Classroom." Drawing from modern science and quality

educational instruction, she has developed a complete model for educational reform. This is a book well worth examining.

(2) Roni Tower wrote a chapter in <u>Imagery: Current theory, research and application</u> (1983). New York: John Wiley & Sons. (pp.222-251). Her chapter, "Imagery: Its role in development" is helpful in understanding imagery as "wired into the human organism." She also describes the environment within which the natural process of imagery can emerge and flourish.

(3) Howard Gardner is a developmental psychologist and Professor of Education at Harvard University's Graduate School of Education. He has written several ground-breaking books on the arts, human development, creativity, and the one most used in <u>Imagine That!</u>: <u>Frames of Mind</u> (1983) New York: Basic Books, Inc.

IMAGERY REFERENCES

The right honorable gentleman is indebted
...to his imagination for his facts.
Richard Brinsley Sheridan

The imagination...gives birth to a system of
symbols, harmonious in themselves ....
Samuel Taylor Coleridge

Achterberg, J. (1985). Imagery in Healing. Boston: Random House. Achterberg was primary in developing imagery within Carl and Stephanie Simonton's cancer research. Her book looks at imagery in healing from a cross-cultural and historical perspective.

Assagioli, R. (1965). Psychosynthesis. New York: Hobbs, Dorman and Co. Roberto Assagioli, an Italian psychiatrist, developed psychosynthesis as a process toward wholeness. The synthesis process uses imagery as a primary teaching process.

Bagley, M. & Hess, K. (1984). 200 Ways to Use Imagery in the Classroom. (3rd ed.). New York: Trillium. This how-to book relates the authors' earlier research on creativity to the many ways to use imagery in schools.

Bandler, R. and Grinder, J. (1975). The Structure of Magic. Palo Alto: Science and Behavior Books, Inc. The first of several volumes "about language and therapy" which formed the foundation of the techniques known as Neuro-Linguistic Programming. This work provides a structure that may be helpful to students of imagery.

Bartlett, J. (1968). Familiar Quotations. Boston: Little, Brown and Co. A good reference book, containing over eleven hundred quotations.

Beebe, R. (1979). Imagery in the Learning Process. Dromenon. 2(3-4), 30-33.*

Benson, H. (1975). The Relaxation Response. New York: Avon. An early book using imagery in stress management and healing.

Bentov, I. (1977). Stalking the Wild Pendulum: On the Mechanics of Consciousness. New York: Bantam Books. The cover states "Now you will have to rethink everything you thought you knew about the nature of reality." A ground-breaking book, it is original, exciting and profound. Our images *do* make a difference!

Bloom, B.S., Englehart, M.B. & Furst, E.J. (Eds.) (1956). Taxonomy of Educational Objectives. Handbook I: Cognitive Domain. New York: Longman. Bloom outlines the structure of instruction for cognition in this volume.

(*Articles from magazines and journals are listed, but not annotated.)

Brain/Mind Bulletin. Published by Interface Press, Box 42211, 4717 N. Figueroa St., Los Angeles, CA 90042. Very good imagery research and reporting.

Bridges, B.R. (1986). Images, Imagination, Creativity and the TMR. Art Education. 39(1), 12-13.

Bronfenbrenner, U. (1979). The Ecology of Human Development. Cambridge, MA: Harvard University Press. Wise, but difficult to read, this book proposes a "curriculum for caring." Bronfenbrenner states that imagistic thought is perhaps the highest form of human thinking.

Calkins, Lucy. (1986). The Art of Teaching Writing. Portsmouth, NH: Heinemann. Calkins' book is indirectly related to imagery studies. It teaches from a naturalistic point of view and uses visual images with young children.

Campbell, Don G. (1983). Introduction to the Musical Brain. Saint Louis: Magnamusic-Baton, Inc. Don was the musician-in-residence when I studied in New York. His work with applications of right brain research to music teaching is "a veritable waterfall of provocative thoughts" (cover).

Capra, F. (1982). The Turning Point. New York: Simon and Schuster. Capra, a physicist, shows us where we have been, where we are, and what human possibilities lie within our reach. It is a very readable book.

Carter, F. (1986). The Education of Little Tree. University of New Mexico Press. A true story, told in images of childhood memory, it captures all the feelings a reader can experience. It shows, through telling stories, how a child's images form and how they last on and on.

Clark, B. (1986). Optimizing Learning. Columbus, OH: Merrill. Clark establishes a model that integrates the best of traditional education with the technologies of the present and the near future. Imagery plays an important role.

Della Neve, C., Hart, L.A., & Thomas, E.D. (1986). Huge Learning Jumps Show Potency of Brain-Based Instruction. Phi Delta Kappan, October.

de Mello, Anthony (1979). Sadhana: a Way to God. St. Louis: The Institute of Jesuit Sources. This was my introduction to meditation. Our group leader was a wonderful woman, a Catholic nun, who taught how Christian exercises in prayer could take Eastern form. Sadhana helped to form my beginning interests in imagery.

Dewey, J. (1938). Experience and Education. New York: Macmillian. This is the classic study of experiential education. Imagery is experiential and builds the kind of quality experiences to which Dewey refers.

Edwards, B. (1979). Drawing on the Right Side of the Brain. Los Angeles: J.P. Tarcher, Inc. Edwards' book shows us a way to implement "right-brain" education, and how the process differs from a traditional approach. I taught drawing from this book for six years. It fostered awarenesses of imagistic thought in my students' lives.

Edwards, B. (1986). <u>Drawing on the Artist Within</u>. This book moves more deeply into inner awareness, focusing upon creativity and the creative process. Imagery parallels this work — often playing an unnamed role.

Eisner, E. (1976) (ed.) <u>The Arts, Human Development and Education</u>. Berkeley: McCutchan Publishing Company. Eisner was one of my "heroes" during my years of teaching art. His knowledge only begins with the arts and expands to tie many educational ideas together.

Epstein, G. (1986). New Model Sees Imagination as Faculty of Inward-Turning Senses. Reported in <u>Brain/Mind Bulletin.</u> 11(10), 1.

Feldenkrais, M. (1972). <u>Awareness Through Movement</u>. New York: Harper and Row. It is amazing to discover what can be learned about the human body, mind and spirit through the processes of this wise teacher.

Ferguson, M. (1980). <u>The Aquarian Conspiracy</u>. Los Angeles: J.P. Tarcher. One of the first real eye-openers for me. If you've not read it, treat yourself to hope for the future. There is a newer edition.

Ferrucci, P. (1982). <u>What We May Be</u>. Los Angeles: J.P. Tarcher.
Ferrucci begins his book with a quotation from Shakespeare: "Lord, we know what we are, but know not what we may be." This is a wonderfully understandable book based upon psychosynthesis practice. Called "techniques for psychological and spiritual growth," it uses imagery in a variety of creative ways.

Fillmer, H.T. & Parkay, F.W. (1985). How Can Hypnosis Improve Reading Proficiency? <u>The Clearing House</u>. 59, 61-63.

Flake, C. (1986). States of Consciousness and Curriculum Development: An Introduction for Teachers. <u>Journal of Humanistic Education.</u> 25(1), 28-37.

Flake, C. (1990). <u>Caring Enough to Teach</u>. Manuscript submitted for publication. Information from the author: Dr. C.L. Flake. Department of Instruction and Teacher Education. University of South Carolina, Columbia, SC 20209. Dr. Flake has written a book that is personal and theoretical. She has filled it with imagery applications.

Fox, Matthew. (1983). <u>Meditations with Meister Eckhart.</u> Santa Fe: Bear & Company. One of a beautiful series of meditational volumes, it is a journey into the richness of imagery as experienced by a Medieval theologian and reported by a contemporary prophet and priest.

Fredericks, A.D. (1986). Mental Imagery Activities to Improve Comprehension. <u>The Reading Teacher.</u> October.

Frey, H. (1980). Improving the Performance of Poor Readers through Autogenic Relaxation Training. <u>The Reading Teacher.</u> 928-932.

Fugitt, Eva D. (1983). <u>He Hit Me Back First: Creative Visualization Activities</u> <u>for Parenting and Teaching</u>. Rolling Hills Estates, CA: Jalmar Press. Fugitt, trained in Psychosynthesis, offers methods to enable children to make quality choices that enhance self-esteem and help them to find their strength and abilities.

Fugitt, Eva D. (1986). Creative Visualization Activities. <u>Day Care and Early</u> <u>Education</u>, Spring, 1986.

Galyean, B. (1980). Meditating with Children: Some Things We Learned. <u>Association for Humanistic Psychology Newsletter</u>. August-September, 16-18.

Galyean, B. (1981). The Brain, Intelligence and Education. <u>Roeper Review</u>, Fall 1981.

Galyean, B. (1982). Science, Human Potential and Education. <u>Institute of</u> <u>Noetic Sciences Newsletter</u>. 10 (1), 6-8.

Galyean, B. (1983a). Guided Imagery in the Curriculum. <u>Educational</u> <u>Leadership</u>. 40 (6), 54-58.

Galyean, B. (1983b). <u>Mind sight</u>. Long Beach (767 Gladys Avenue): Center for Integrative Learning. This is her seminal effort and it is a very special book that contains imagery exercises for all ages.

Galyean, B. (1983c). The Use of Guided Imagery in Elementary and Secondary Schools. <u>Imagination, Cognition and Personality</u>. 2 (2), 145-151.

Galyean, B. (1985). Guided Imagery in Education. In A.A. Sheikh (Ed.), <u>Imagery in Education</u>. Farmingdale, NY: Baywood. This book is a part of the Imagery and Human Development Series and may be ordered through the AASMI (American Association for the Study of Mental Imagery).

Gardner, H. (1983). <u>Frames of Mind: The Theory of Multiple Intelligences.</u> New York: Basic Books. Gardner's theory of multiple intelligences presents a means for educators to reach all children and guide them into the development of their potentials. Ground-breaking, this book establishes "a whole new way of looking at human beings."

Gardner, H. (1986). <u>The Mind's New Science</u>. New York: Basic Books. Howard Gardner, a distinguished research scientist, devotes an entire chapter in this book to imagery as he tells the story of the cognitive revolution.

Ghiselin, B. (1952). <u>The Creative Process</u>. Berkeley, CA: University of California Press. In telling the stories of the creative geniuses of our century, Ghiselin documents their individual statements and approaches to imagistic thought.

Goldberg, Natalie. (1986). Writing Down the Bones: Freeing the Writer Within. Boston: Shambhala. I look for images and in Goldberg's work, they are abundant in another imagery application, writing.

Goldberg, Philip. (1983). The Intuitive Edge: Understanding Intuition and Applying It in Everyday Life. Los Angeles: Tarcher Press. Goldberg is informative and helpful toward a deeper understanding of intuition.

Greeson, L. & Zigarmi, D. (1985). Piaget, Learning Theory and Mental Imagery: Toward a Curriculum of Visual Thinking. Humanistic Education and Development. 24 (1), 40-49.

Hammer, S. (1984). The Mind as Healer. Science Digest. 92 (4), 46-49, 100.

Hampden-Turner, Charles. (1981). Maps of the Mind. New York: Macmillan. A brilliant compendium of major "maps" of the human mind.

Harmon, W. (1983). The President's Letter. From The Institute of Noetic Science. November 21, 1983.

Harmon, W. & Rheingold, H. (1984). Higher Creativity. New York: Longman. This outstanding book contains a chapter on imagery. Harmon is director of the Institute of Noetic Sciences.

Hendricks, G. & Roberts, T. (1977). The Second Centering Book. Englewood Cliffs, NJ: Prentice Hall, Inc. Tom Roberts was one of my mentors and this book is one of my favorites. It contains many imagery exercises and one of the most complete subject bibliographies I've ever seen.

Holt, R.R. (1964). Imagery: The Return of the Ostracized. American Psychologist. 19 (4), 254-264.

Houston, J. (1979). Through the Looking-Glass: The World of Imagery. Dromenon. 2 (3-4), 17-25.

Jaffe, D.T. & Bresler, D.W. (1980). Guided Imagery: Healing Through the Mind's Eye. In Shorr, J. (Ed.), Proceedings of the first annual conference of the American Association for the Study of Mental Imagery.

James, William. (1958). The Varieties of Religious Experience. New York: The New American Library, Inc. Producing the passionate images he believed necessary, James' is the classic book on the psychology of religion.

Johnson, E., Sickels, E., & Sayers, F.C. (1959). Anthology of Children's Literature. Boston: Houghton Mifflin Company. This is a book I have used for many years with my students, my children and now my grandchildren. It contains good children's books, poems, etc. and has illustrations by N.C. Wyeth.

Johnson, R.A. (1986). Inner Work. New York: Harper and Row. Johnson, a priest and Jungian analyst, uses clear yet symbolic imagery in explaining and using his method of personal growth processes.

Keirsey, D. and Bates, M. (1984). Please Understand Me: Character & Temperament Types. Del Mar, CA: Prometheus Nemesis Book Company. Based upon Jung's personality types, this book offers further understanding of ways of thinking, learning and being in the world.

Kelsey, Morton T. (1976). The Other Side of Silence: A Guide to Christian Meditation. New York: Paulist Press. With this book, used by my minister in a Sunday School class, I began my meditational practice. It offers "help for those who have doubts about the possibility, or the value, of meditation."

Khatena, Joe (1984). Imagery and Creative Imagination. Buffalo: Bearly Limited. This book is worth noting because his approach differs from others. It is a beginning model for the measurement of and focus on the relationship between imagery and creativity.

Lazarus, A. (1977). In the Mind's Eye: The Power of Imagery for Personal Enrichment. New York: Rawson. This one explains imagery, its power and how to use it for self-growth.

Lewis, R. (1984). Reaffirmations: Speaking Out for Children. A Child's Right to Imagine. Young Children. 39 (5), 82.

Longino, L.R. (1987). Imagery practice for teachers of young children: An ethnographic study of perceptions of change. (Doctoral dissertation, University of South Carolina, Columbia, SC, 1987). Dissertation Abstracts International. This is my complete imagery research study. Part of the basic information in this book, Imagine That!, comes from this study.

Lovgren, G.K. (1977). Sustaining and Encouraging Visual Imagery in Children Prior to Learning to Read. Reading Improvement, 14 (4), 268-74.

Maltz, Maxwell (1960). Psychocybernetics. New York: Prentice Hall. Maltz introduced many of us to the idea of self-image. It is worth reading to see the progress made in the past thirty years.

Masters, Robert. (1983). Psychophysical Method Exercises. Pomona, NY: A Dragon Book. A student of G. I. Gurdjieff and Milton Erickson, Masters combines the bodyworks of Moshe Feldenkrais and F. Matthias Alexander with his own innovative techniques. His work incorporates imagery and is powerful and effective.

Masters, R. and Houston, J. (1978). Listening to the Body: The Psychophysical Way to Health and Awareness. New York: Dell Publishing Co. This is a book of theory and practice that is helpful in understanding how to use inner images to "correct...habits of mind and movement."

Masters, R. and Houston, J. (1972). Mind Games. New York: Dell Publishing Co. Written by my mentors, I used the powerful and innovative imagery exercises in this book to lead my first adult groups.

May, Rollo. (1975). The Courage to Create. New York: W.W. Norton. An important lesson to be learned on the road toward creative expression: Courage is not the absence of fear and despair, but the ability to make choices and move on in spite of them! It is a visionary and passionate book.

McKim, R.H. (1972). Experiences in Visual Thinking. Boston: Wadsworth. McKim's book was my early introduction to "visual thinking" and creativity. He shows the interactions between seeing, imagining, and drawing.

Murdock, M. (1981). Spinning Inward. Culver City, CA: Peace Press. A recently revised edition is available through Shambhala Press. This is a valuable source for guided imagery exercises. They are organized around specific subject matter in the curriculum for learning, creativity and relaxation.

Noetic Sciences Bulletin. Published by the Institute of Noetic Sciences. 475 Gate Five Road, Suite 300, PO Box 909, Sausalito, CA 94966-0909.

Nouwen, Henri J.M. (1974). Out of Solitude. Notre Dame, IN: Ave Maria Press. Nouwen's writings greatly influenced me. Each meditation is full of images that are powerful and gentle.

On the Beam. A newsletter published by New Horizons for Learning, an International Human Relations Network, Seattle, WA 98103. This newsletter was begun by creative educators in the northwest. I recommend network membership for parents and educators interested in the newest means and methods of learning.

O'Regan, B. (1982). The Puzzle of Untapped Potentials. Institute of Noetic Sciences Newsletter. 10 (1), 1, 18-20.

Ostrander, S. and Schroeder, L.(1979). Superlearning. New York: Dell Publishing Co. This book encourages the examination of personal participation in accessing abilities and creating health and self-esteem. It uses imagery exercises as a part of a plan to increase potentials in adults and children.

Paivio, A. (1971). Imagery and Verbal Processes. New York: Holt. Paivio establishes the relationship between the image and the word as dual and complementary processes.

Parrott, C.A. & Strongman, K.T. (1985). Utilization of visual imagery in creative performance. Journal of Mental Imagery. 9(1), 53-66.

Pelletier, K.R. (1977). Mind as Healer, Mind as Slayer. New York: Dell Publishing Co. A building-block in the foundation of the self-health industry, Pelletier's book outlines his training and research methodology to provide strong evidence for the role of stress in illness.

Progoff, Ira. (1975). At a Journal Workshop. New York: Dialogue House Library. Fortunate to be able to attend a Progoff journal workshop, I learned how to journal in this "intensive process."

Prather, Hugh. (1981). A Book of Games: A Course in Spiritual Play. New York: Doubleday & Co. I have enjoyed many of Prather's books. Beautiful, gentle, inspirational images seem to dance throughout this one.

Pressley, G.M. (1976). Mental Imagery Helps Eight-Year Olds Remember What They Read. Journal of Educational Psychology. 68(3), 355-359.

Rheingold, H. (1982). Imagination and the Importance of Daydreaming. Institute of Noetic Sciences Newsletter. 10 (1), 4-5, 20.

Rico, G.L. (1983). Writing the Natural Way. Los Angeles: J.P. Tarcher. I learned the process of "clustering" in a workshop under Rico. It is a right-brain process related to imagery, well-taught in this book.

Roberts, T. (1981). Consciousness, Psychology and Education. Journal of Transpersonal Anthropology. 5(1), 79-100.

Roberts, T. (1985). States of Consciousness: A New Intellectual Direction, a New Teacher Education Direction. Journal of Teacher Education. 36 (2), 55-59.

Rockenstein, Z. (1985). A Taxonomy of Educational Objectives for the Intuitive Domain. (Doctoral dissertation, University of Georgia, Athens, GA, 1985). Dissertation Abstracts International. (University Microfilms No. 8514035). Rockenstein offers a broad picture of how imagery supports intuition in this good sourcebook.

Rose, R. (1979). A Program Model for Altering Children's Consciousness. The Gifted Child Quarterly. 23(1), 109-117.

Rosen, S. (Ed.) (1982). My Voice Will Go With You: The Teaching Tales of Milton H. Erickson. New York: W.W. Norton and Company. This warm and revealing book about creative processes in hypnotherapy, clarifies Erickson's reputation for wit and insight.

Rossman, M.L. (1987). Healing Yourself: A Step-by-Step Program for Better Health through Imagery. New York: Walker & Co. This book is full of information on how to get started in an imagery-based health program

Samples, Bob. (1976). The Metaphoric Mind. Menlo Park: Addison-Wesley. This book is a classic, a book "in which all of our inner capacities are honored and celebrated."

Satir, Virginia (1972). Peoplemaking. Palo Alto: Science and Behavior Books, Inc. Satir's work has so infused the psychological literature that it is interesting to note what is her original work.

Seldes, George (Ed.) (1985). The Great Thoughts. New York: Ballantine Books. This is a helpful reference book. Use it to find out who said what, or just thumb through it for insightful quotations.

Shames, R. and Sterin, C. (1978). Healing with Mind Power. Emmaus, PA. Rodale Press. This book, my introduction to self-healing, uses imagery ("guided meditation") to help gain control of one's life.

Sheikh, A.A. & Sheikh, K.S. (Eds.) (1985). Imagery in Education. Imagery and Human Development Series, Farmingdale, NY: Baywood Publishing Company, Inc. This is a compilation of articles by some of today's outstanding researchers of imagistic thought.

Siegel, B.S. (1986). Love, Medicine & Miracles. New York: Harper & Row. This very popular book is by a doctor willing to challenge traditional medical practice to help his patients take control of their living.

Simonton, D.C., Matthews-Simonton, J. S. & Creighton, J.S. (1978). Getting Well Again. New York: Bantam Books. This book shows how patients can partner with their doctors and use imagery in healing.

Singer, D. and Singer, J. (1985). Make Believe: Games and Activities to Foster Imaginative Play in Young Children. Glenview, IL: Scott, Foresman and Company. Jerome Singer is one of the foremost researchers in imagistic thought. He is one of the few researchers who can conduct research, report theory, and write on an understandable level.

Spangler, David. (1984). Emergence: The Rebirth of the Sacred. Spangler says we are seeing the beginnings of "a new covenant between God and the wholeness of planetary life." His images are beautiful. His fervor and passion offer the kind of hope that the qualitative practice of imagery can provide.

Stewart, D. (1985). Teachers Aim at Turning Loose the Mind's Eye Smithsonian. 16(5), 44-53.

Thompson, M.L. (1983). Think Before You Write: Using Guided Imagery in the Classroom. Curriculum Review. October. 37-39.

Vaughn, F. (1979). Awakening Intuition. New York: Doubleday. Vaughn states that imagery is the language of intuition. She led the way in reminding readers of the importance of intuition as a way of knowing.

Vitale, Barbara Meister. (1986). Free Flight: Celebrating Your Right Brain. Rolling Hills Estates, CA: Jalmar Press. Using applications of right brain methods in her life, Vitale shares her experiences in learning. She supports those for whom the Logical-Mathematical world of education failed to meet their needs.

Vitale, Barbara Meister. (1982). Unicorns Are Real: A Right-Brained Approach to Learning. Rolling Hills Estates, CA: Jalmar Press. Vitale's book outlines a creative approach for parents and educators who want to work together to promote a better education for children.

von Oech, Roger.(1983).   A Whack On the Side of the Head. New York: Warner.   This book presents a wonderful adventure. I used it to encourage creative thinking in high school art classes. It is effective and it's FUN!

Wachs, H. (1981).   Visual Implications of Piaget's Theory of Cognitive Development. Journal of Learning Disabilities. 14 (10), 581-3.

SUGGESTED AUDIOTAPES

The Golden Voyages series by Bearns and Dexter. Awakening Productions. Culver City, CA 90230.

Paul Winter's works (especially Common Ground and Canyon) Living Music Records. Sausalito, CA 94965.

Kitaro's works (especially Tunhuang and India). Manufactured in Germany.

George Winston's works (practically all of them).

Pachelbel's Canon (available in many various recordings). Listen for your favorite version.

The Environments series. I like Slow Ocean and Wind.

Prelude to Lazaris by Steven Boone. Concept: Synergy. Fairfax, CA 94930.

Andreas Vollenweider's works (especially White Winds). CBS Records, New York, NY.

Steven Halpern's works (such as Spectrum Suite). Halpern Sounds. Belmont, CA 94002.

Don Campbell's works. For a complete listing, write to: Institute for Music, Health & Education. Post Office Box 1244, Boulder, CO 80306.

There are countless wonderful sounds to accompany imagery! An important consideration is to allow the music to support the exercise and not compete or overpower it. Concentration, or focus, is important in learning to practice imagery and too insistent or too loud a selection of music can interfere. Good choices are available at every record/tape shop.

ABOUT THE AUTHOR

Lane Longino Waas has a Master's Degree in the Visual Arts and a Ph.D. in Early Childhood and Teacher Education. Her interest in imagery grew out of sixteen years as an art educator, three years of training at the Foundation for Brain and Mind Research and the successful use of healing imagery with her daughter's spinal injury. She has designed courses for and guided adult imagery groups, worked with imagery students of all ages and conducted workshops and seminars for state and national professional groups. Lane currently lives in Florida and conducts workshops on imagery nationwide. She has four grown children and two grandchildren.

Learning The Skills of Peacemaking
An Activity Guide for Elementary-Age Children

"Global peace begins with you. Guide develops this fundamental concept in fifty lessons. If this curriculum was a required course in every elementary school in every country, we would see world peace in our children's lifetimes." — *Letty Cottin Pogrebin*, Ms. Magazine
0-915190-46-X $21.95
8½ × 11   paperback, illus.

The Two Minute Lover
Announcing A New Idea In Loving Relationships

No one is foolish enough to imagine that s/he *automatically* deserves success. Yet, almost everyone thinks that they automatically deserve sudden and continuous success in marriage. Here's a book that helps make that belief a reality.
0-915190-52-4 $9.95
6 × 9   paperback, illus.

Feel Better Now
30 Ways to Handle Frustration in Three Minutes or Less
Most of us realize that letting go of tension is a key to happiness and health. This book explains the dynamics of letting go.

0-915190-66-4 $9.95
6 X 9   paperback

Good Morning Class—I Love You!
Thoughts and Questions About Teaching from the Heart

A book that helps create the possibility of having schools be places where students, teachers and principals get what every human being wants and needs—LOVE!

0-915190-58-3 $6.95
5½ × 8½ paperback, illus.

Unlocking Doors to Self-Esteem

Presents innovative ideas to make the secondary classroom a more positive learning experience—socially and emotionally—for students and teachers. Over 100 lesson plans included. Designed for easy infusion into curriculum. Gr. 7-12

0-915190-60-5 $16.95
6 × 9 paperback, illus

Project Self-Esteem EXPANDED
A Parent Involvement Program for Elementary-Age Children

An innovative parent-support program that promotes children's self-worth. "Project Self Esteem is the most extensively tested and affordable drug and alcohol preventative program available."

0-915190-59-1 $39.95
8½ × 11   paperback, illus.

Reading, Writing and Rage

An autopsy of one profound school failure, disclosing the complex processes behind it and the secret rage that grew out of it.

Must reading for anyone working with learning disabled, functional illiterates, or juvenile delinquents.

0-915190-42-7 $16.95
5½ × 8½ paperback

Esteem Builders

You CAN improve your students' behavior and achievement through building self-esteem. Here is a book packed with classroom- proven techniques, activities, and ideas you can immediately use in your own program or at home.

Ideas, ideas, ideas, for grades K-8 and parents.

0-915190-53-2 $39.95
8½ × 11   paperback, illus.

I am a blade of grass
A Breakthrough in Learning and Self-Esteem

Help your students become "lifetime learners," empowered with the confidence to make a positive difference in their world (without abandoning discipline or sacrificing essential skill and content acquisition).
0-915190-54-0 $14.95
6 × 9   paperback, illus.

SAGE: *Self-Awareness Growth Experiences*

A veritable trove of activities and strategies promoting positive behavior and meeting the personal/social needs of young people in grades 7-12. Organized around affective learning goals and objectives. Over 150 activities.
0-915190-61-3   **$16.95**
6 × 9 paperback, illus.

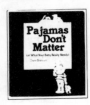

Pajamas Don't Matter:
(or What Your Baby Really Needs)

Here's help for new parents everywhere! Provides valuable information
and needed reassurances to new
parents as they struggle through the
frantic, but rewarding, first years of
their child's life.
0-915190-21-4 $5.95
8½ × 11 paperback, full color

Why Does Santa Celebrate Christmas?

What do wisemen, shepherds and
angels have to do with Santa,
reindeer and elves? Explore this
Christmas fantasy which ties all of
the traditions of Christmas into one
lovely poem for children of all
ages.
0-915190-67-2 $12.95
8 1/2 x 11 hardcover, full color

Feelings Alphabet

Brand-new kind of alphabet book full
of photos and word graphics that will
delight readers of all ages.". . .lively,
candid . . .the 26 words of
this pleasant book express
experiences common to all children."
Library Journal
0-935266-15-1 $7.95
6 × 9 paperback, B/W photos

The Parent Book

A functional and sensitive guide for
parents who want to enjoy every minute of their child's growing years.
Shows how to live with children in
ways that encourage healthy emotional development. Ages 3-14.
0-915190-15-X $9.95
8½ × 11 paperback, illus.

Aliens In My Nest
SQUIB Meets The Teen Creature

Squib comes home from summer
camp to find that his older brother,
Andrew, has turned into a snarly,
surly, defiant, and non-communica-
tive adolescent. *Aliens* explores the
effect of Andrew's new behavior on
Squib and the entire family unit.
0-915190-49-4 $7.95
8½ × 11 paperback, illus.

Hugs & Shrugs
The Continuing Saga of SQUIB

Squib feels incomplete. He has lost a
piece of himself. He searches every
where only to discover that his missing piece has fallen in and not out.
He becomes complete again once
he discovers his own inner-peace.

0-915190-47-8 $7.95
8½ × 11 paperback, illus.

Moths & Mothers/
Feather & Fathers
*A Story About a Tiny Owl
Named SQUIB*

Squib is a tiny owl who cannot fly.
Neither can he understand his feelings. He must face the frustration,
grief, fear, guilt and loneliness that
we all must face at different times in
our lives. Struggling with these feelings, he searches, at least, for
understanding.

0-915190-57-5 $7.95
8½ × 11 paperback, illus.

Hoots & Toots & Hairy Brutes
*The Continuing Adventures
of SQUIB*

Squib—who can only toot—sets out
to learn how to give a mighty hoot.
His attempts result in abject failure.
Every reader who has struggled with
life's limitations will recognize their
own struggles and triumphs in the
microcosm of Squib's forest world. A
parable for all ages from 8 to 80.

0-915190-56-7 $7.95
8½ × 11 paperback, illus.

Do I Have To Go To School Today?
Squib Measures Up!

Squib dreads the daily task of going
to school. In this volume, he
daydreams about all the reasons he
has not to go. But, in the end, Squib
convinces himself to go to school
because his teacher accepts him
"Just as he is!"

0-915190-62-1 $7.95
8½ × 11 paperback, illus.

The Turbulent Teens
Understanding Helping Surviving

"This book should be read by every
parent of a teenager in America. . .It
gives a parent the information
needed to understand teenagers and
guide them wisely."—Dr. Fitzhugh
Dodson, author of *How to Parent,
How to Father, and How to Discipline
with Love.*
0-913091-01-4 $8.95
6 ⅛ 9 paperback.

Openmind/Wholemind
Parenting & Teaching Tomorrow's Children Today

A book of powerful possibilities that honors the capacities, capabilities, and potentials of adult and child alike. Uses Modalities, Intelligences, Styles and Creativity to explore how the brain-mind system acquires, processes and expresses experience. Foreword by M. McClaren & C. Charles.
0-915190-45-1 $14.95
7 × 9   paperback
81 B/W photos   29 illus.

Present Yourself! *Captivate Your Audience With Great Presentation Skills*

Become a presenter who is a dynamic part of the message. Learn about Transforming Fear, Knowing Your Audience, Setting The Stage, Making Them Remember and much more. Essential reading for anyone interested in the art of communication. Destined to become the standard work in its field.
0-915190-51-6   paper $9.95
0-915190-50-8   cloth $18.95
6 × 9   paper/cloth. illus.

Unicorns Are Real
A Right-Brained Approach to Learning

Over 100,000 sold. The long-awaited "right hemispheric" teaching strategies developed by popular educational specialist Barbara Vitale are now available. Hemispheric dominance screening instrument included.
0-915190-35-4 $12.95
8½ × 11   paperback, illus.

Unicorns Are Real Poster

Beautifully-illustrated. Guaranteed to capture the fancy of young and old alike. Perfect gift for unicorn lovers, right-brained thinkers and all those who know how to dream. For classroom, office or home display.

JP9027 $4.95
19 × 27   full color

Imagination is the unicorn that lifts us above the mundane chains that bind the minds of many and flies us on fantastic wings to a place where dreams DO come true.

Practical Application, Right Hemisphere Learning Methods

Audio from Barbara Vitale. Discover many practical ways to successfully teach right-brained students using whole-to-part learning, visualization activities, color stimuli, motor skill techniques and more.
JP9110 $12.95
Audio Cassette

Don't Push Me, I'm Learning as Fast as I Can

Barbara Vitale presents some remarkable insights on the physical growth stages of children and how these stages affect a child's ability, not only to learn, but to function in the classroom.
JP9112 $12.95
Audio Cassette

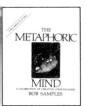

Metaphoric Mind (Revised Ed.)

Here is a plea for a balanced way of thinking and being in a culture that stands on the knife-edge between catastrophe and transformation. The metaphoric mind is asking again, quietly but insistently, for equilibrium. For, after all, equilibrium is the way of nature.
0-915190-68-0 $14.95
7 x 10 paperback, B/W photos

Free Flight *Celebrating Your Right Brain*

Journey with Barbara Vitale, from her uncertain childhood perceptions of being "different" to the acceptance and adult celebration of that difference. A book for right-brained people in a left-brained world. Foreword by Bob Samples.
0-915190-44-3 $9.95
5½ × 8½   paperback, illus.

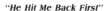

"He Hit Me Back First"
Self-Esteem through Self-Discipline

Simple techniques for guiding children toward self-correcting behavior as they become aware of choice and their own inner authority.
0-915190-36-2 $12.95
8½ × 11   paperback, illus.

Learning To Live, Learning To Love

An inspirational message about the importance of love in everything we do. Beautifully told through words and pictures. Ageless and timeless.
0-915190-38-9 $7.95
6 × 9   paperback, illus.

TA For Tots
(and other prinzes)
Over 500,000 sold.

This innovative book has helped
thousands of young children
and their parents to better
understand and relate to each
other. Ages 4-9.
0-915190-12-5 $12.95
8½ × 11 paper, color, illus.

TA For Tots, Vol. II

Explores new ranges of
feelings and suggests
solutions to problems
such as feeling hurt,
sad, shy, greedy, or
lonely.
Ages 4-9.
0-915190-25-7 $12.95
8½ × 11 paper, color, illus.

TA For Tots Coloring Book

Constructive, creative coloring
fun! The charming *TA For Tots*
characters help show kids that
taking care of their feelings is
OK! Ages 2-9.
0-915190-33-8 $1.95
8½ × 11 saddle stitched, illus.

TA Today I'm OK Poster

Cheerful, happy TA creatures
help convey the most positive,
upbeat message to be found.
Perfect for brightening your
room or office.
JP9002 $3.00
19 × 27 full color poster

TA for Kids
(and grown-ups too)
Over 250,000 sold.

The message of TA is presented
in simple, clear terms so
youngsters can apply it in their
daily lives. Warm Fuzzies
abound. Ages 9-13.
0-915190-09-5 $9.95
8½ × 11 paper, color, illus.

TA For Teens
(and other important people)
Over 100,000 sold.

Using the concepts of Transac-
tional Analysis. Dr. Freed
explains the ups and downs of
adulthood without talking down
to teens. Ages 13-18.
0-915190-03-6 $18.95
8½ × 11 paperback, illus.

Original Warm Fuzzy Tale
*Learn about "Warm Fuzzies"
firsthand.*
Over 100,000 sold.

A classic fairytale. . .with adventure, fantasy, heroes, villains
and a moral. Children (and
adults, too) will enjoy this beautifully illustrated book.
0-915190-08-7 $7.95
6 × 9 paper, full color, illus.

Songs of The Warm Fuzzy
"All About Your Feelings"

The album includes such songs
as Hitting is Harmful, Being
Scared, When I'm Angry,
Warm Fuzzy Song, Why
Don't Parents Say What
They Mean, and I'm Not
Perfect (Nobody's Perfect).
JP9003R/C $12.95
             Cassette

Tot Pac *(Audio-Visual Kit)*

Includes 5 filmstrips, 5 cas-
settes, 2 record LP album. A
Warm Fuzzy I'm OK poster, 8
coloring posters, 10 Warm Fuz-
zies. 1 *TA for Tots* and 92 page
Leader's Manual. No prior TA
training necessary to use Tot
Pac in the classroom! Ages 2-9.
JP9032 $150.00
Multimedia program

Kid Pac *(Audio-Visual Kit)*

Teachers, counselors, and parents of pre-teens will value this
easy to use program. Each *Kid
Pac* contains 13 cassettes, 13
filmstrips, 1 *TA For Kids*, and a
comprehensive *Teacher's Guide*,
plus 10 Warm Fuzzies. Ages
9-13.
JP9033 $195.00
Multimedia Program